A Students AutoCAD

Antoine Briand
Queens University
Electronic engineering
September 1988 - June 1993

IAN MILLIKEN.
73 UPPER ROAD,
GREENISLAND.

A Students AutoCAD

A. Yarwood

Longman
Scientific &
Technical

Longman Scientific & Technical,
Longman Group UK Limited,
Longman House, Burnt Mill, Harlow,
Essex CM20 2JE, England
and Associated Companies throughout the world.

Copublished in the United States with
John Wiley & Sons, Inc., 605 Third Avenue, New York, NY 10158

© Longman Group UK Limited 1991

First published 1991

British Library Cataloguing in Publication Data
Yarwood, A. (Alfred) 1917–
  A students AutoCAD.
  1. Technical drawings. Draftsmanship. Applications of
computer systems
  I. Title
  604.2402854

Library of Congress Cataloging-in-Publication Data
Yarwood, A. (Alf)
    A student's AutoCAD/A. Yarwood.
      p.   cm.
    Includes index.
    ISBN 0–470–21704–9 : £7.95
    1. AutoCAD (Computer program)   I. Title.
  T385.Y37   1991
  620'.0042'02855369–dc20

                                                    90–48743
                                                    CIP

Set in Melior (Linotron 202)
Produced by Longman Singapore Publishers (Pte) Ltd.
Printed in Singapore

Contents

List of Plates (between pages 146 and 147)

Preface

This book is intended for use by those who wish to learn how to produce technical drawings with the aid of the computer software package AutoCAD. AutoCAD is the world's most widely used computer-aided design (CAD) software package. This means that more computer workstations throughout the world are equipped with AutoCAD than with any other CAD package. AutoCAD is a software package with a host of facilities, some of which are not discussed in this book. This book, however, contains sufficient information on how to use AutoCAD for producing technical drawings to satisfy the requirements of students in the upper forms of schools and in further and in higher education. It will also be a valuable text for those in industry new to CAD and who wish to learn how to use and familiarise themselves with AutoCAD.

AutoCAD is a complex drawing and design tool. Because of this, no attempt is made within the pages of this book to describe its more advanced facilities. For example, the host of variables which can be set by entering the **setvar** command system are not described; the use of macros to speed up some of the processes of drawing with the software is not included. There is, however, sufficient information and exercise material to enable students to undertake the production of complicated technical drawings of an advanced nature. It is hoped that, as skill in the use of AutoCAD advances, the reader will find he/she is able to experiment with facilities in the software not described here and to undertake further reading and research from information gained from the large number of books dealing with this remarkable CAD package.

All the drawings in this book were drawn with the aid of AutoCAD, working with an Epson PC. All drawings, except one, were plotted with the aid of a Roland plotter. The exception was printed with the aid of an Epson dot matrix printer.

AutoCAD release II

As this book was being published, AutoCAD release 11 was released. This book does not cover the more advanced systems of AutoCAD but its contents are suitable for use by readers working with release 11. Those using release 11 will note that the on-screen and pull-down menus contain more commands than those of release 10, but all the methods of drawing described in this book can be carried out when working with release 11.

To ensure compatibility between release 10 and release 11, a variable – **TILEMODE** – has been introduced in release 11. TILEMODE can be **ON** (set at 1) or **OF** (set at 0).

When a drawing constructed in release 10 is loaded into release 11, TILEMODE is automatically set to ON and release 11 then acts as if it were release 10. This means that drawings constructed in release 10 can be loaded into release 11. If the release 10 drawing is then saved while in release 11, the TILEMODE setting of ON is saved with the drawing.

The AutoCAD command system

To call or select commands when constructing drawings in AutoCAD any one of the following systems may be used, depending upon the equipment available with the workstation at which one is working:

1. Typing the name of a command at the keyboard;
2. Selecting (or calling) a command by *pointing* at its name in the appropriate *on-screen* menu with the aid of a mouse or puck;
3. Selecting a command by pointing at its name in the appropriate *pull-down* menu with the aid of a mouse or puck;
4. Selecting a command by pointing at its name on a graphics tablet overlay with a puck or stylus.

In this book, when a command system is outlined, three words are used to describe the actions involved in selecting and taking constructive action with the commands. These are:

Keyboard – the letters, word(s) or figures are to be typed in from the keyboard;

Return – either press the *Return* key of the computer keyboard, or the key of the mouse or puck which acts as a *Return* key;

Pick – press the *pick* button of the pointing device in use – mouse, puck or stylus.

If working entirely from the keyboard without the assistance of a mouse, puck or stylus, all commands must be typed in from the keyboard and the *Return* key must be used as a *pick* as well as a *Return* key.

Note: Throughout the pages of this book commands from AutoCAD are shown in either capital or in lower-case letters. This is because, when using this software, commands and responses can be keyed in either capitals or lower-case letters.

Acknowledgements

The author wishes to record here his appreciation of the help given by representatives of the Education and Training Department of Autodesk Limited, the UK office of the producers of AutoCAD, and in particular, his gratitude for the technical advice offered by Andrew Lancaster of Autodesk Limited, after his reading of the draft text and drawings of this book.

In addition the author wishes to thank the following: his son-in-law, Tom Droy, for introducing him to computing many years ago and always being available for technical assistance with computing problems; Brian Davies of Imperial College, London, a co-author of two other books on computing, for advice and assistance on matters concerned with education and computing in higher education; and members of the staff of the Salisbury College of Technology, for introducing him to AutoCAD in the first place.

AutoCAD, AutoLISP, and AutoShade are registered trademarks of Autodesk Inc.

MS.DOS is a registered trademark of the Microsoft Corporation.

IBM is a registered trademark of the International Business Machine Corporation.

A. Yarwood is a Registered Applications Developer for AutoCAD with Autodesk.

CHAPTER 1

Introduction

Scope of this book

This book has been written to give students in schools and colleges
an introduction into CAD (computer-aided drawing) with the aid of
the software package AutoCAD. Note that the term 'CAD' can have
at least two meanings — computer-aided drawing (or draughting)
and computer-aided design. In this book the term 'CAD' is used in
its computer-aided drawing (draughting) sense.

AutoCAD is not difficult to use for straightforward drawing.
AutoCAD is, however, a very complex drawing tool with possibilities well beyond the needs of students in educational establish-
ments. With this in mind, only the more common methods of
drawing with its aid are described in detail. The less commonly
used methods are described only in outline.

There are a number of different versions of AutoCAD. This book
describes the use of:

1. MS.DOS release 10 AutoCAD, or later, software;
2. IBM or IBM compatible PC (personal computer) with:
    (a) at least 640 kbytes of RAM (random access memory);
    (b) an EGA (enhanced graphics adaptor) or VGA (video
         graphics adaptor) card and the appropriate monitor;
    (c) a suitable maths coprocessor (8087, 80287 or 80387);
    (d) a hard disc on which the AutoCAD files are stored.

Note: All exercises in these pages, except those in Chapters 10
and 11, can also be worked with version 9 of the software. The
exercises can also be worked with other computer set-ups.

Starting up AutoCAD on a PC

When a PC is switched on, a file — *autoexec. bat* — automatically
loads files from the hard disc into the computer memory.

Depending upon how this *autoexec. bat* file has been written, the computer will:

1. Load some files into memory so that AutoCAD can immediately be used, or;
2. Load instructions on to the monitor screen stating how AutoCAD can be loaded, or;
3. Respond with a prompt such as **C:>**. If this prompt appears, typing *ACAD* (or *acad*) and then pressing the *Return* key at the keyboard, normally loads the software ready for use.

When the necessary AutoCAD files have been loaded, a list of eight numbered options headed **Main menu** appears:

Main menu

0. Exit AutoCAD
1. Begin a NEW drawing
2. Edit an EXISTING drawing
3. Plot a drawing
4. Printer Plot a drawing

5. Configure AutoCAD
6. File Utilities
7. Complete shape/font description file
8. Convert old drawing file

Enter selection:_

Of the options 1 to 8, choose

1. Begin a NEW drawing

and type the figure 1 in answer to the query

Enter selection: 1 *keyboard Return*

which appears at the bottom of the screen.

A further prompt

Enter NAME of drawing:_

then appears.

A name, e.g. *draw\01*, should be typed in response to this prompt.

In the given response *draw* is the name of the directory in which drawing files can be kept on the hard disc and *01* the name given to the drawing about to be produced on screen.

Notes: The directory *draw* must first be made (with the

MS.DOS command *md* or *mkdir*) on the hard disc of the PC before
entering AutoCAD.

If an AutoCAD drawing file is seen in its directory, as e.g. when
giving MS.DOS command *dir* when not in AutoCAD, it will be
found to have the extension *.dwg*. Thus the file *01* in directory
draw will have a full title of *draw\01.dwg*.

The drawing editor of AutoCAD

When the name of a new drawing has been entered in response to
the **Enter NAME of drawing:** prompt, pressing the *Return* key of the
computer brings the *drawing editor* on to the monitor screen. The
screen will then appear somewhat like Fig. 1.1. The screen is
divided into four areas:

1.   A drawing area;
2.   A status line;
3.   A command line;
4.   An on-screen menu area.

The exact appearance of the drawing editor screen will depend
partly on how the software has been configured and partly on how
the *acad.mnu* (later automatically compiled to *acad.mnx*) has been
written.

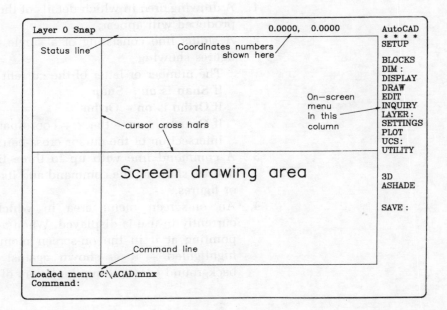

Fig. 1.1 The drawing editor
screen of AutoCAD

The screen may appear as suitable for drawing in millimetres on an A4 size drawing sheet; on an A3 size sheet; with or without borders; with or without a title block; in other sheet sizes and configurations. The drawing editor screen for a new drawing is configured under the option

5. Configure AutoCAD

of the **Main menu** and following the subsequent prompts when *Return* has been pressed. In the example given (Fig. 1.1), the initial drawing set-up produced a screen suitable for an A3 size drawing sheet, with limits of 420, 297 (the dimensions in millimetres of an A3 sheet), with a **SNAP** size of 10 (**on**), and coordinates (**off**). Items like limits, **snap** sizes, **grid** sizes, **snap on/off**, **grid on/off** and other such details can be amended as required – see pp. 98–101.

The drawing editor screen

A typical drawing editor screen appears as in Fig. 1.1. In some AutoCAD computer equipment set-ups, two monitor screens, one to display the drawing currently being worked and the other to contain the command menus, will be seen. Such a set-up allows for a larger drawing area. The more common set-up is as in Fig. 1.1, with a single monitor screen.

The drawing editor consists of four parts:

1. A *drawing area* in which details of the drawing currently being produced will appear;
2. A *status line* consisting of a single line of letters, words or figures showing:
    The number or letter of the current layer;
    If **Snap** is **on** – Snap
    If **Ortho** is **on** – Ortho
    If **Coords** is **on** – the x, y coordinates of the position of the intersection of the cursor cross-hairs.
3. A *command line* with up to three lines of words, letters or figures, showing the command and its associated words, letters or figures;
4. An *on-screen menu* area in which the command menu currently in use is displayed. When a command is selected by pointing at it in the on-screen menu area, the command is *highlighted* – it is shown against a rectangular coloured background surrounding the letters of the command.

Drawing in the drawing editor

With the aid of the set-up dealt with here – PC, EGA or VGA monitor, coprocessor and AutoCAD version 10 (or later) – drawings are constructed by positioning the intersection of the cursor cross-hairs on screen with the aid of one of the following types of pointing device:

1. *The four arrow cursor keys* – up, down, left and right. Pressing the *Page Up* key speeds up the action of the cursor keys, pressing *Page Down* slows down the action of the cursor keys. Confirmation of the position of the cursor intersection is made by pressing the *Return* key of the keyboard;
2. *A mouse*. Mouse devices may have one, two or more keys. If the mouse possesses at least two keys, one can be used as a *pick* key for confirming (picking) a position, the other for acting as a *Return* key to switch back to **Command:** on the prompt line of the drawing editor. More than two keys allows the keys of a mouse to be configured for a variety of commands – e.g. key 3 could be the *redraw* key, key 4 could be an **erase** key;
3. *A graphics tablet*. Graphics tablets can be configured to allow a number of commands to be entered when the cross-hairs of a puck, or the point of a stylus, are pointed at a command entered on an overlay on the graphics tablet. The command overlays can be simple as in Fig. 1.2 or can be as complex as the whole of the command menus of AutoCAD. A puck may have as many as twelve keys, each of which can be configured to give a separate command when pressed. On the other hand pucks may have only two or three keys.
4. *A trackerball or a joystick* – either of which device can be used in much the same way as is a mouse.

The two most commonly used devices for controlling the cursor cross-hairs and for selecting commands from menus are a mouse or a graphics tablet with puck or stylus. Both have their advantages. Some operators prefer using a mouse for some drawing operations and a graphics tablet for other operations. Occasionally the arrow cursor keys can be used to advantage in conjunction with any of the other pointing devices.

Command selection

A major feature of AutoCAD is its command structure. The selection of commands determines what is to be drawn or what is

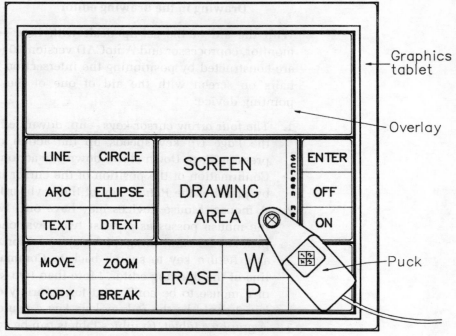

Fig. 1.2 A simple graphics tablet overlay with a puck

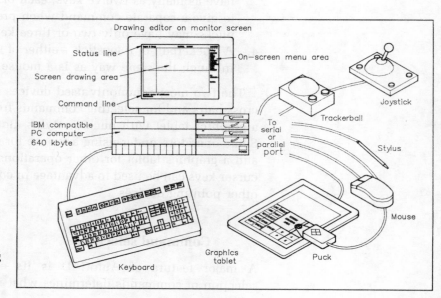

Fig. 1.3 The various pointing devices which can be used with AutoCAD

to appear in the screen drawing area of the monitor. The commands consist of words or abbreviations which are displayed on screen in *menus* and *sub-menus* (*nested menus*). In addition, *dialogue boxes* can be called to the screen from some of the commands. Examples of menus, sub-menus and dialogue boxes will appear in the pages of this book.

Commands can be selected in a variety of ways determined partly by the type of pointing device being operated with the set-up:

1. By pressing the *Insert* key of the computer keyboard and then the arrow cursor keys to move up and down the menu to highlight a required command. Pressing the *Return* key of the computer brings the highlighted command into operation;
2. By pointing at the required command with the aid of a mouse. The intersection of the cross-hairs of the cursor are moved by the mouse into the on-screen menu area. Moving the mouse up and down the menu area will highlight each command in turn. When the required command has been highlighted, pressing the mouse *pick* button brings the command to the command line;
3. By placing the cross-hairs of a puck or the point of a stylus over a command printed on a graphics tablet overlay. Pressing the *pick* button of the pointing device brings the command into operation;
4. By selecting from the screen menu area of a graphics tablet (Fig. 1.2). As the pointer is moved up and down, the on-screen area commands will be highlighted. Selection of the required command is again made by pressing the pointing device *pick* button. Note that as the puck cross-hairs are moved over the screen drawing area of the graphics tablet overlay, so the cursor cross-hairs will move correspondingly over the drawing area of the monitor screen;
5. From the *pull-down menus* associated with version 9 and later versions of AutoCAD. If the pointing device moves the cursor into the area of the status line, menu prompts will appear on the status line. Pointing at one of these prompts and pressing the *pick* button brings down the pull-down menu associated with the picked prompt. Figure 1.4 shows the **Draw** menu of a typical pull-down menu system;
6. By keying in the command from the computer keyboard. The command appears on the command line. Any figures, letters or words required to use the command can also be keyed in.

In practice a variety of these methods may be put into operation.

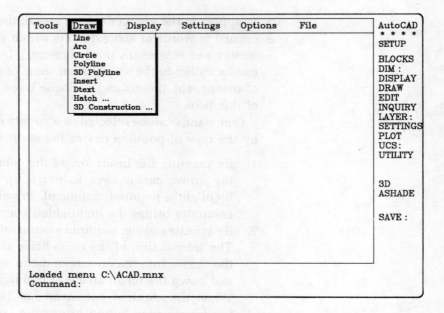

Tools	Draw	Display	Settings	Options	File	AutoCAD

```
Line
Arc
Circle
Polyline
3D Polyline
Insert
Dtext
Hatch ...
3D Construction ...
```

```
* * * *
SETUP

BLOCKS
DIM :
DISPLAY
DRAW
EDIT
INQUIRY
LAYER :
SETTINGS
PLOT
UCS :
UTILITY

3D
ASHADE

SAVE :
```

```
Loaded menu C:\ACAD.mnx
Command:
```

Fig. 1.4 A pull-down menu
from AutoCAD

For example, if working mainly with a mouse as a pointing device, some commands may be selected from the on-screen menu area, some from the pull-down menus and some by keying in commands at the keyboard.

Note on examples of commands in this book

Throughout this book, the given examples of command usage are as if they have been selected from the on-screen menu or keyed in at the command line from the keyboard. Operators may, however, prefer selecting some commands from the pull-down menus or, if a graphics tablet is in use, the method of selecting of commands from the menus on the tablet overlay may be preferred.

Coordinates

The Cartesian coordinate system of AutoCAD is basically two-dimensional (2D) with units along x, y axes. When the software's three-dimensional (3D) system is actuated a further z axis comes into operation (pp. 110–113). Under normal operating conditions, the bottom left-hand corner of the drawing editor is x, $y = 0, 0$. The coordinate point at the top right of the screen drawing editor will vary according to the setting of the **LIMITS** command. If, for example, the screen drawing editor has been set as for an A3 size sheet, the top right-hand point will be x, $y = 420, 297$.

x, y coordinates are positive to right and upwards and negative to left and downwards.

The coordinate system can be switched **on** and **off** (toggled) by pressing the function key f6. When f6 is pressed, the state of the coordinate system shows up at the command line (bottom) of the drawing editor, either as <**Coords on**> or <**Coords off**>, whichever applies. If **Coords** are **on**, the position of the cursor cross-hairs in *x, y* numbers is constantly updated at the status line (top) of the drawing editor as the cursor is moved by the pointing device. A further control of **Coords on/off** is given by pressing keys *Control* (*Ctrl*) and *D*. If **Coords** is **on**, pressing *Ctrl+D* changes the *x, y* units as shown at the status line from showing *absolute* positions of the cursor to showing *relative* positions – and vice versa. If **Coords** is **off**, pressing *Ctrl+D* switches **Coords on**. Further examples of *Ctrl+letter* toggles are given below.

Two examples of *x, y* coordinate numbers as they appear at the status line when lines are being drawn in the drawing editor are shown in Fig. 1.5.

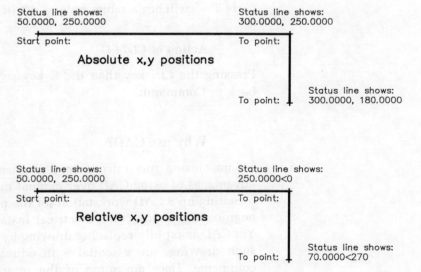

Fig. 1.5 Absolute and relative
x, y coordinates

In Fig. 1.5, the upper drawing shows the numbers appearing at the status line giving the absolute (the actual) *x, y* positions at the ends of the lines as each point is picked. In the lower drawing the *x, y* coordinate numbers relative to the last point picked show up at the status line. In the number 250.0000<0, for example, the figure 250 gives the unit length of the line from the **First point:** position, and <0 gives the angle (<) in degrees, measured anticlockwise from a line which is horizontal and to the right of the position from which the measurement is taken.

Further information about drawing lines to unit lengths is given in Chapter 2.

Action of the function keys

f1 – flips between drawing editor screen and information screen;
f6 – switches **Coords on** or **off**;
f7 – switches **Grid** dots **on** or **off**;
f8 – switches **Ortho on** or **off**;
f9 – switches **Snap on** or **off**;
f10 – switches a graphics tablet **on** or **off** (if in use);

Other toggles:

Ctrl+B – switches **SNAP on** and **off**;
Ctrl+D – switches **ORTHO on** and **off**;
Ctrl+G – switches **GRID on** and **off**;
Ctrl+O – switches **ORTHO on** and **off**;
Ctrl+T – switches a tablet **on** and **off** (if one is in use).

Action of *Ctrl+C*

Pressing the *Ctrl* key then the *C* key switches the command line back to **Command:**.

Why use CAD?

Before closing this introductory chapter, a few words about the advantages of using CAD over manual methods are appropriate.

Setting up a CAD workstation for the production of drawings for engineering, architecture, electrical installation, etc. is expensive. Yet CAD is rapidly replacing drawing by hand in situations where such drawings are essential – in education, in industry and in commerce. Here are some of the reasons why CAD is rapidly replacing hand methods:

1. Drawings can be produced much more rapidly with CAD equipment. Depending upon the work in hand, a speed of as much as 10 times faster can be achieved. With some types of drawing, in which details have to be repeatedly copied, speeds in excess of this are possible;

2. Drawing with CAD equipment is less tedious than drawing by

hand. Tedious drawing processes such as printing notes and filling in hatched areas can be drawn in with CAD software quickly, accurately and easily without tedium;

3. The same detail need never be drawn twice. Any drawing detail can be moved, copied, rotated, scaled or inserted into any drawing. Any drawing can be inserted into another drawing to any scale and/or position required. A rule to which all CAD operators should adhere is:

    Never draw the same thing twice

4. Drawings can be saved as disc files and so stored on discs for recall when needed. This means that it is virtually unnecessary to have a store of drawings on paper, tracing or whatever. This entails a great saving of space where hundreds or thousands of drawings are constantly being called for. Any drawing from a disc file can be plotted or printed to any scale when required;

5. New details can be added to a drawing with ease. Details can be deleted or amended without having to redraw a whole drawing. This is particularly important as a time-saving device in firms where constant design updating is important;

6. CAD drawings produced by skilled draughtsmen are more accurate than those produced by hand. In fact some of the automatic drawing features of CAD such as dimensioning reduces the possibility of errors creeping into drawings.

All this does not mean that skill in draughtsmanship is no longer needed. In fact the same draughting/design skills are required by CAD operators as before, but in addition, they must also be skilled in the use of the computer systems into which their CAD software is loaded.

Exercises

1. What is meant by 2D Cartesian coordinates?
2. What is meant by the terms:
    Absolute coordinates?
    Relative coordinates?
3. Give three methods by which details such as lines can be drawn in the AutoCAD drawing editor.
4. Name the different types of pointer device which can be used to draw in the drawing editor of AutoCAD.
5. Name the various parts of the screen as it appears when a new drawing or the editing of an existing drawing is commenced.
6. Explain why it is that CAD is replacing drawing by hand in

most industrial companies.

7. Six of the f (function) keys have special uses in AutoCAD. Name them.

8. When drawing in the AutoCAD drawing editor, what happens when the following keys are pressed?
   (i)   *Ctrl+B*;
   (ii) *Ctrl+D*;
   (iii) *Ctrl+G*;
   (iv) *Ctrl+O*;
   (v)   *Ctrl+T*.

CHAPTER 2

Frequently used drawing commands

Introduction

The majority of drawings produced with the aid of CAD software consist mostly, some entirely, of straight lines, circles, arcs and text. In AutoCAD such commands are held in the **DRAW** menu. In this menu, each of the individual commands has its own sub-menu (nested menu). Two such sub-menus as shown in Fig. 2.1, which shows the on-screen menu areas for four sub-menus connected with the **DRAW** menu.

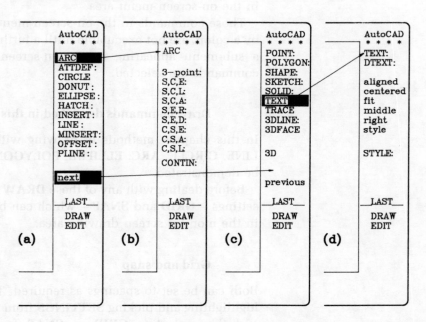

Fig. 2.1 Details from the on-screen **DRAW** menu

In Fig. 1.1, when the **DRAW** command is highlighted in the on-screen menu area and picked by pointing and then pressing the *pick* button of the pointing device, Fig. 2.1(a) appears, listing some of the commands within the **DRAW** menu. If **next** is then

highlighted and picked, Fig. 2.1(c) appears with the remainder of
the **DRAW** commands.

Each of the commands in the **DRAW** menu has its own sub-
menu. Two such sub-menus are shown in Fig. 2.1. If **ARC** is
highlighted and picked (Fig. 2.1(a)), Fig. 2.1(b) appears showing the
methods by which arcs can be drawn within the drawing editor. If
TEXT is highlighted and picked (Fig. 2.1(c)), Fig. 2.1(d) appears,
showing that either **TEXT** or **DTEXT** (dynamic text) can be chosen,
together with the positions possible for placing the text on screen.

On-screen menu commands

Those commands appearing in the on-screen menu which are
followed by a colon (:) are immediately executable. When a
command name followed by a colon is selected, the command is
repeated at the command line, together with appropriate prompts.
A sub-menu of prompts associated with the command also appears
in the on-screen menu area.

Those commands in the on-screen menu which are not followed
by a colon, are not executable until a further selection is made from
a sub-menu appearing in the on-screen menu area when such
commands are selected.

Draw commands described in this chapter

In this chapter, methods of drawing with the **DRAW** commands
LINE, **CIRCLE**, **ARC**, **ELLIPSE**, **POLYGON**, **PLINE** and **TEXT** will
be demonstrated.

Before dealing with any of these **DRAW** commands, there are two
settings – **GRID** and **SNAP** – which can be of value when drawing
in the monitor screen drawing area.

Grid and snap

Both can be set to spacings as required. They can be set either by
highlighting and picking **SETTINGS** from the main on-screen menu
and then selecting **GRID** or **SNAP** from the sub-menu which
appears, or the commands can be keyed in at the keyboard.

When **GRID** is selected the following appears at the command
line of the drawing editor:

Command: GRID
Grid spacing(X) or ON/OFF/Snap/Aspect<0.0000>:

If 10, say, is keyed into this prompt and the *Return* key pressed, a grid of dots with vertical and horizontal intervals of 10 units will appear on screen as in Fig. 2.2.

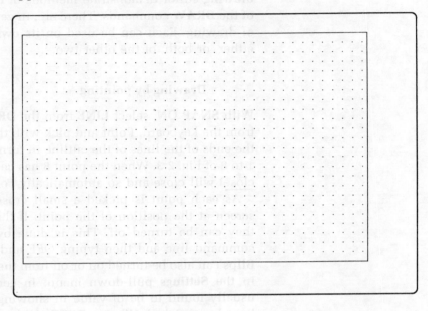

Fig. 2.2 The drawing editor screen with grid points

When **SNAP** is selected the following appears at the command line:

> **Command: SNAP**
> **Snap spacing or ON/OFF/Aspect/Rotate/Style/<1.0000>:**

Keying in, say 10, at the keyboard sets the snap spacings at intervals of 10 units vertically and horizontally.

When **SNAP** is **ON**, the intersection of the cursor cross-hairs automatically locks (snaps) on to the nearest snap point. This enables the operator to achieve great accuracy in positioning the cursor.

The variety of possible settings which appear for either **grid** or **snap** (e.g. **A**spect, **S**tyle, etc.) will be explained in later pages.

Grid can be switched **ON** or **OFF** by pressing the function key f7; **Snap** can be switched **ON** or **OFF** by pressing function key f9.

GRID and **SNAP** need not be set to the same numbers – e.g. **Grid** could be set at 10 and **Snap** set at 5.

Note: **GRID** and **SNAP** can also be set from the **Drawing Aids** . . . option in the **Settings** pull-down menu.

The command LINE

The following descriptions of producing lines in the screen drawing editor demonstrate methods of drawing common to many of the **DRAW** commands. There are, in general, three main methods of drawing. Each can be used on its own, or in conjunction with either, or both, of the other two.

Drawing by pointing

With **SNAP ON**, select **LINE** from the **DRAW** menu, or key in *line* from the keyboard. Point and pick with the pointing device each of the ends of the lines of the outline in turn – e.g. following the order 1 to 8 of Fig. 2.3. When the point 8 has been picked, keying in *c* (for close) will *close* and so automatically complete the outline.

As each point is picked a small cross (a *blip*) appears on the screen at the position of the point. If these blips are not wanted, they can be turned off. This is done by typing **blipmode** at the command line and then typing *OFF* and pressing the *Return* key. Blips can also be turned on or off from the **Drawing Aids** . . . option in the **Settings** pull-down menu. In general, however, blips are usually found to be of value in showing on screen which points have been picked. When a **REDRAW** is called, the blips disappear as the screen is refreshed and redrawn.

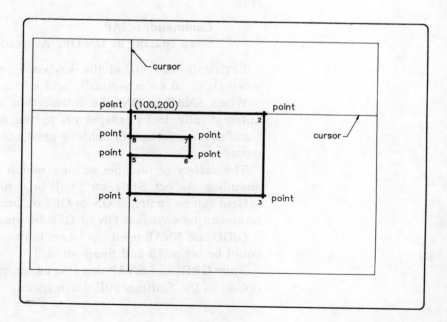

Fig. 2.3 Drawing by picking points with the **LINE** command

Drawing by stating coordinates

In Fig. 2.4, select **LINE** from the **DRAW** menu, or key in *line* from the keyboard. Then, to obtain a required outline, key in the x, y coordinate figures of the ends of the lines in turn, following the prompts as follows:

    Command: LINE
    From point: 100, 200   *Return*
    To point: 250, 200   *Return*
    To point: 250, 120   *Return*

and so on until the outline has been completed.

Typing c at the x, y position 100, 180 of Fig. 2.4 will complete the outline automatically.

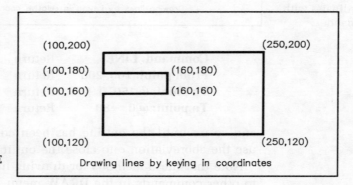

Fig. 2.4 Drawing by keying in coordinates with the **LINE** command

Drawing by relative coordinates

The precise unit length of lines can be accurately drawn by the method of keying in relative coordinates (Fig. 2.5). If the relative coordinate numbers are required to show on the status line of the drawing editor screen, press function key f6 to switch **coords on**. Then key in the relative coordinate numbers prefixing the unit lengths with the symbol @. Note that:

Lines drawn to the right are positive;
Lines drawn to the left are negative;
Lines drawn upwards are positive;
Lines drawn downwards are negative.

Thus the responses to the prompts on the command line will follow the pattern:

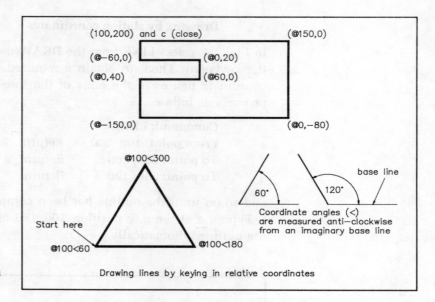

Fig. 2.5 Drawing by keying in relative coordinates with the **LINE** command

Inside figure:
(100,200) and c (close)   (@150,0)
(@−60,0)   (@0,20)
(@0,40)   (@60,0)
(@−150,0)   (@0,−80)

@100<300
Start here
@100<60   @100<180

base line
60°   120°
Coordinate angles (<) are measured anti−clockwise from an imaginary base line

Drawing lines by keying in relative coordinates

Command: LINE	*Return*
From point: 100, 200	*Return*
To point: @150, 0	*Return*
To point: @0, −80	*Return*

and so on until the outline has been completed, remembering to use the abbreviation *c* to close the outline.

Note that these methods for drawing lines apply equally as well to other commands in the **DRAW** menu.

Figure 2.5 also shows lines being drawn to relative coordinates at angles to each other. Note that the angles must be measured in degrees *anticlockwise* to an imaginary line running to the right of the point about which the line is to be drawn. To draw to relative coordinates to give lines at angles other than 90° to each other, the symbols @ and < precede the length of line and the angle (anticlockwise) around 0°.

The command CIRCLE

Select **CIRCLE** from the **DRAW** menu and the screen will appear as in Fig. 2.6. Circles can be drawn by first defining the circle centre by picking or by keying in the centre coordinates (followed by pressing the *Return* key) and then either picking or keying in the units of the **Radius (R)** or **Diameter (D)**.

If a circle passing through **2points** or through **3points** is required

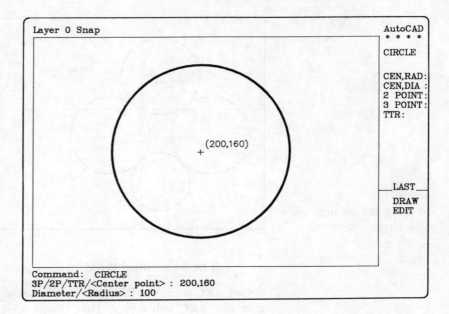

```
Layer 0 Snap                                          AutoCAD
                                                      * * * *
                                                      CIRCLE

                                                      CEN,RAD:
                                                      CEN,DIA :
                                                      2 POINT:
                                                      3 POINT:
                                                      TTR:

                        (200,160)
                       +

                                                      LAST
                                                      DRAW
                                                      EDIT

Command:   CIRCLE
3P/2P/TTR/<Center point> : 200,160
Diameter/<Radius> : 100
```

Fig. 2.6 Drawing a circle
with the **CIRCLE** command

then select one of these from the **CIRCLE** sub-menu. After picking
or keying in the coordinates of the 2 or 3 points, the required circle
will appear.

If circles tangential to one another, to lines, to arcs or tangential
to lines and arcs or circles, are needed, first draw the lines, arcs and
circles to which other circles are to be tangential. Then select **TTR**
(tangent, tangent, radius) from the **CIRCLE** sub-menu. The following will appear on the command line:

Command: CIRCLE	*Return*
3P/2P/TTR/<Center point>:ttr	*Return*
Enter Tangent spec:	*point with pointing device*
Enter second Tangent spec:	*point*
Radius: *state required radius Return*	

and the tangential circle will appear on screen.

When using the **ttr** prompt, the required radius can be given by
pointing at two points anywhere on the screen indicating the length
of the radius.

Figure 2.7 shows two circles of radius 40 units tangential to two
other circles. This method of drawing circles tangential to each
other is of good value when drawing a shape such as that shown on
the right of Fig. 2.7, which was developed from the four tangential
circles on the left of Fig. 2.7.

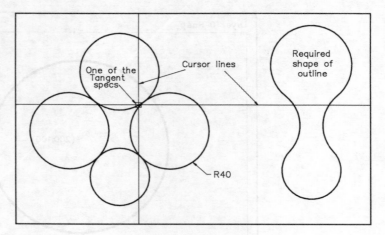

Fig. 2.7 Using the **ttr** prompt
of the **circle** command

The command ARC

Select **ARC** from the **DRAW** menu. The on-screen menu changes to
give the **ARC** sub-menu. This shows that arcs may be drawn by
choosing any three parameters from the list shown in Fig. 2.8. The
parameters are indicated in the sub-menu by initial letters. To give
an example of the drawing of an arc, choosing Centre, Start, End
(C, S, E) from the sub-menu:

Command: ARC
Center/<Start point>: C:
Center: *pick (or key in coordinates)*
Start point: *pick (or key in coordinates)*
Angle/Length of chord/<End point>: DRAG *pick*
(or key in coordinates)

and the required arc appears on screen in the drawing editor. The
other three-initial arc prompts are as easy to follow – make sure
you are following the prompts in the command line.

Examples of the methods by which arcs can be drawn are given
in Fig. 2.8.

Notes

1. Arcs will normally appear on screen being drawn in an
   anticlockwise direction;
2. The **ttr** (tangent, tangent, radius) prompt of the **circles**
   command allows circles to be drawn tangentially to any arc.

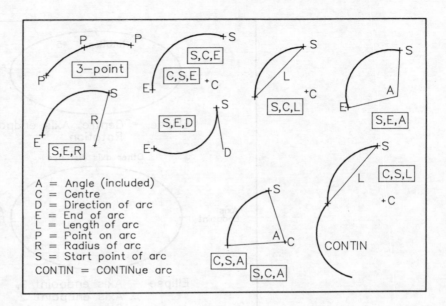

A = Angle (included)
C = Centre
D = Direction of arc
E = End of arc
L = Length of arc
P = Point on arc
R = Radius of arc
S = Start point of arc
CONTIN = CONTINue arc

Fig. 2.8 The prompts from
the **ARC** menu

The command ELLIPSE

There are three principal methods of drawing ellipses. A fourth –
isometric ellipses – only applies when the drawing editor is set up
for isometric drawing. Two of the methods are shown in Fig. 2.9:

1. Upper drawing of Fig. 2.9:

    Command: ELLIPSE
    <Axis endpoint 1>/Center: c *Keyboard Return*
    Center of ellipse: *pick (or key in coordinates)*
    Axis endpoint: *pick (or key in coordinates)*
    <Other axis distance>/Rotation: r *Keyboard Return*
    Rotation around major axis: 45 *Keyboard Return*

    and the required ellipse will appear on screen.
    Note: The **Rotation** option allows ellipses to be drawn as if
    the minor axis of the ellipse has been rotated around the major
    axis by an angle equal to the stated figure in degrees.

2. Lower drawing of Fig. 2.9:

    Command: ELLIPSE
    <Axis endpoint 1>/Center: *pick axis endpoint 1*
    Axis endpoint 2: *pick axis endpoint 2*
    <Other axis distance>/Rotation: *pick distance Return*

    and the required ellipse will appear on screen.

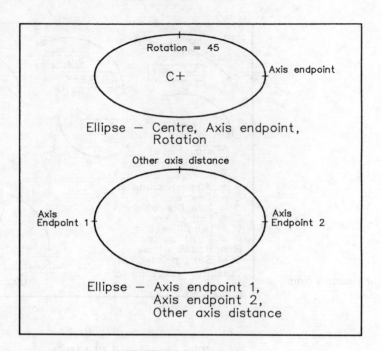

Fig. 2.9 Methods of drawing ellipses

The command POLYGON

POLYGON is another command from the **DRAW** menu (see Fig. 2.10). When it is selected, the command line of the drawing editor shows

> **Command: POLYGON Number of sides:** 6 *(say) Keyboard Return*
> **Edge/<center of polygon>:** *pick* **Inscribed in circle/Circumscribed around circle (I/C):** i *Keyboard Return*
> **Radius of circle:** *pick (or number)*

and the polygon appears on screen. Or

> **Command: POLYGON Number of sides:** 8 *(say) Return*
> **Edge/<center of polygon>:** *pick* **Second end point of edge:**
> *pick*

and the polygon appears on screen.

Notes

1. When the **polygon** command is used, when the polygon appears on screen, the positions of its vertices will not be fixed until either the *pick* button of the pointing device is pressed or

the *Return* key of the keyboard is pressed. The polygon can thus be drawn, e.g. standing on a base, or standing on one of its vertices.

2.　All polygons drawn with the **polygon** command are *regular*, i.e. all sides are equal and all angles are the same size.

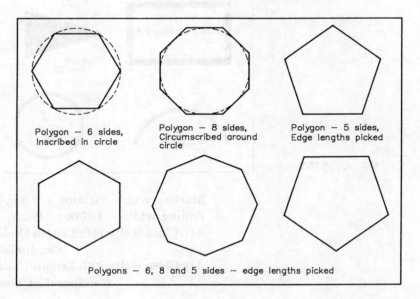

Fig. 2.10 Drawing polygons

The command PLINE

When constructing a drawing on screen which includes both thick and thin lines, the thick lines can be drawn as *polylines* or **PLINE**s. These are produced in much the same way as are **LINE**s, except that the thickness of a **pline** can be established before it is drawn. Straight **pline**s and arc **pline**s can be drawn from the **pline** command structure. Circles can be constructed from two semicircle arc **pline**s. Figure 2.11 shows examples of **pline** lines and arcs.

Note: All parts of a polyline are treated as a single object until *Return* is pressed twice at the same ending point or until the polyline is closed with the prompt *c* (close).

When **PLINE** is called the command line shows

Command: PLINE
From point: *pick*
Current width is 0.0000
Arc/Close/Halfwidth/Length/Undo/Width/
　　　　　　　<endpoint of line>: w *Keyboard Return*

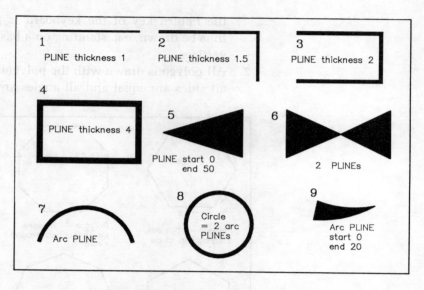

Fig. 2.11 Various **PLINE**s

Starting width <0.0000>: 1 *Keyboard Return*
Ending width <1.0000>: *Return*
Arc/Close/Halfwidth/Length/Undo/Width/
 <endpoint of line>: *pick end point*
Arc/Close/Halfwidth/Length/Undo/Width/
 <endpoint of line>: *pick second end point*

repeats until *Return* or polyline is closed with *c*.

Command:

The command TEXT

If text is to be added to drawings, the command **style** is first called
to determine the *style* of text to be drawn. The AutoCAD software
package contains a number of text files, some of which are shown
in Fig. 2.12. When first drawing in the drawing editor, the text style
in use will probably be the *Standard* font. To change to another text
style, use the **STYLE** command.

To change to another text style, e.g. *Complex*, select **STYLE** by
typing or selecting with the pointing device. The following then
appears at the command line:

Command: STYLE *Return*
Text style name (or ?): <STANDARD>: complex *Keyboard*
 Return
New style.
Font file <txt>: complex *Keyboard Return*

> **Height <0.0000>**: 8 *(say) Return*
> **Width factor <1.00>**:   *Return*
> **Obliquing angle <0>**:   *Return*
> **Backward? <N>**:   *Return*
> **Upside-down? <N>**:   *Return*
> **Vertical? <N>**:   *Return*
> **COMPLEX is now the current text style.**

Each prompt can be answered by a *Y* or a number to alter the aspect of the selected font.

Figure 2.12 shows examples of some of the text styles available with standard AutoCAD software and the aspects available if the aspect prompts are answered with other than pressing the *Return* key of the keyboard.

With the **style** command, different fonts can be loaded ready to use as **text** for printing letters or figures in the AutoCAD drawing editor. When **style** is called, the font in use can be changed, its HEIGHT; its WIDTH; its *OBLIQUING ANGLE*; its position BACKWARDS; ᑌᑭƧIᗡE–ᗡOWᴎS; or V
E
R
T
I
C
A
L can be changed or chosen.

AutoCAD fonts in common use are: SIMPLEX; STANDARD (TXT); COMPLEX; *ITALIC*; MONOTXT.

Other fonts can be chosen, among which are: ROMANS; ROMAND; ROMANC; *ITALICC*; *ITALICT*; 𝒮𝒸𝓇𝒾𝓅𝓉𝒸; 𝒮𝒸𝓇𝒾𝓅𝓉𝓈; 𝕲𝖔𝖙𝖍𝖎𝖈𝖊; 𝕲𝖔𝖙𝖍𝖎𝖈𝖌; 𝕲𝖔𝖙𝖍𝖎𝖈𝖎; Greek and Cyrillic fonts, and also symbols for Astronomy, Mapping, Mathematics, Meteorology and Music.

Fig. 2.12 The variety of text styles possible with AutoCAD

When the command **TEXT** is selected the following appears on the command line:

> **Command: TEXT** *Return*
> **Start point or Align/Center/Fit/Middle/Right/Style:** *pick*
> **Height <0.0000>**: 0 *Keyboard Return*
> **Rotation angle <0>**:   *Return*
> **Text:** *type in required text*   *Return*

Note: If **DTEXT** (dynamic text) is selected, the text appears on screen as it is being typed. With the **TEXT** command, text does not appear on screen until it has been typed at the command line and then the *Return* key pressed.

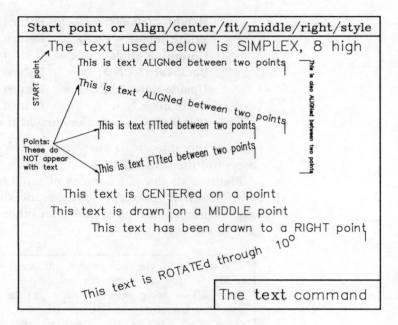

Fig. 2.13 Adding text with the **TEXT** command

The command OSNAP

Accuracy in drawing is achieved with the aid of **GRID** and **SNAP**. Another set of commands which will assist accurate drawing are the **OSNAP** (object snap) group.

OSNAP commands can be selected from the **Tools** pull-down menu or by pointing and picking the four stars (****) appearing just under the name **AutoCAD** in the on-screen menu. The **OSNAP** series allow the operator to snap on to details such as the **END**points, the **INT**ersections, **TAN**gential points, (among others) of elements in a drawing.

When an **OSNAP** command is chosen a *pick box* appears at the junction of the cursor cross-hairs. Depending upon which of the **OSNAP** commands is selected, the line, arc, circle, etc. being drawn snaps on to the appropriate position within the pick box — e.g. **END**point, the **INT**ersection point or the **MID**point. Figure 2.14 shows the **OSNAP** prompts in the **Tools** pull-down menu.

Answering and saving exercises

The software files for AutoCAD will be held on the computer's hard disc. Answers to exercises in this book can be **SAVE**d to a floppy disc held in drive a: of the computer. This floppy disc could be labelled *WORK DISC* and could be used to hold all the drawings

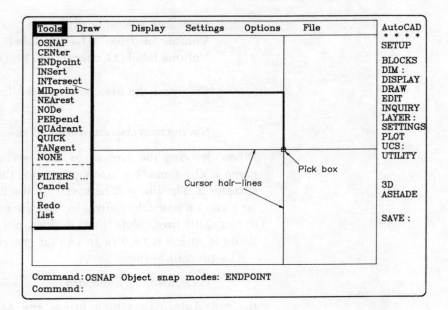

Fig. 2.14 The **Tools** pull-down menu showing the object **snap** commands

made while working through this book. Depending on the type of floppy disc in use, several may be required by the time all the drawings for exercises in this book have been completed.

Caution

When working with AutoCAD it is advisable first to construct an answer to an exercise in a drawing file on the hard disc. When the answer has been completed, then **SAVE** it to the floppy disc. Also, if an exercise answer previously **SAVE**d to a floppy disc is to be amended in any way, it is advisable first to copy its drawing file from the floppy to the hard disc (see p. 169). When the amendments have been made, then **SAVE** the file to the floppy disc.

All this may seem somewhat of a chore, but working a drawing file in AutoCAD from a floppy disc is a much slower process than working it from a hard disc. Also, AutoCAD writes details under construction to a series of temporary files, which are automatically deleted when a drawing is **SAVE**d. If a floppy disc is nearly full when a drawing file is about to be **SAVE**d, there is a possibility of crashing out of AutoCAD and losing the drawing being constructed.

Preparing a work disc

At the **C:\\>** prompt type:

C:\\>label a: *Keyboard Return*
Volume in drive A has no label
Volume label (11 characters, ENTER for none)?– work_disc
Keyboard Return
C:\\> *and the disc now has the label WORK DISC*

Saving exercise answers to disc

When drawing the answer to an exercise, each answer could be given a file name, e.g. *a:\\chap2_01* for the answer to Exercise 1 of Chapter 2. The file will be saved on the floppy disc in drive a: and be given an extension *.dwg*, so that the complete file name will be *a:\\chap2_01.dwg*. Note that it does not matter whether the file name is in lower-case or in capital letters.

The procedure therefore is

C:\\> acad   *Keyboard)*

to load AutoCAD, which brings the **Main menu** on screen. In response to:

1. Begin a NEW drawing
Enter selection: 1   *Keyboard*
Enter NAME of drawing: chap2_01   *Keyboard Return*

and the AutoCAD drawing editor appears on screen ready for you to create your drawing answer.

When the drawing answer has been completed it can be saved by calling the command **SAVE**:

Command: Save   *Keyboard Return*
File name <A:\\CHAP2_01>:   *Return*
Command:

and the file is saved to the disc in drive a: as a file with the name *a:\\chap2_01.dwg*, the extension *.dwg* being added automatically.

Plotting or printing a drawing

If, at this stage you wish to produce *hard copy* – plots or prints – of your drawings, turn to Chapter 12, where the processes necessary for printing or plotting are described.

Exercises

The following exercises will give practice with the commands:

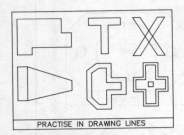

Fig. 2.15 Exercise 1

LINE, CIRCLE, ARC, ELLIPSE and POLYGON. It is assumed that they will be drawn in the AutoCAD drawing editor with LIMITS set to 420, 297 (A3 size sheet in mm), with GRID at 10 and SNAP at 5. Do not include any dimensions.

1.   Figure 2.15 shows some outlines drawn with the LINE command. Copy the given outlines to any sizes you find suitable.

2.   Figure 2.16 shows three drawing outlines which have been dimensioned. Draw the given outlines to the stated dimensions. Do not include the dimensioning.

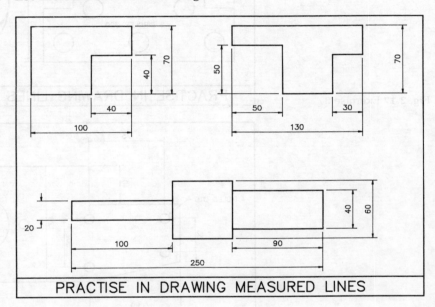

PRACTISE IN DRAWING MEASURED LINES

Fig. 2.16 Exercise 2

3.   The outlines of five shapes which include circles are given in Fig. 2.17. Using the LINE and CIRCLE commands, draw the given outlines to the dimensions given. Do not attempt to include the dimensions in your drawing.

4.   Figure 2.18 is a drawing of a fixing tab. Copy the drawing to the given sizes. Do not include the dimensions

5.   Figure 2.19 shows four drawings with circles, constructed with the aid of the ttr prompt of the circle command, tangentia to lines and other circles. Copy the drawings using the same commands.

The drawings for exercises 6–12 are given in Fig. 2.20.

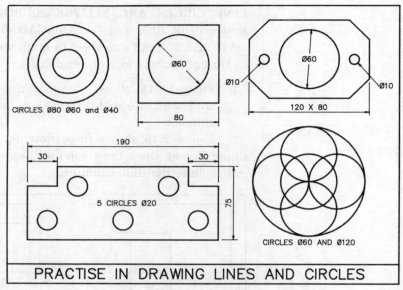

Fig. 2.17 Exercise 3

CIRCLES Ø80 Ø60 and Ø40

Ø60

80

Ø60

Ø10   Ø10

120 X 80

190

30   30

5 CIRCLES Ø20

75

CIRCLES Ø60 AND Ø120

PRACTISE IN DRAWING LINES AND CIRCLES

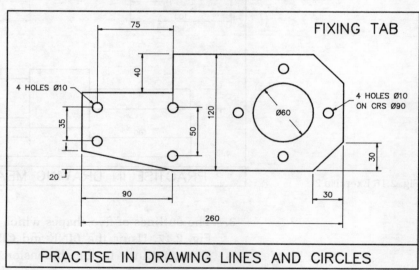

Fig. 2.18 Exercise 4

75

40

FIXING TAB

4 HOLES Ø10

120

Ø60

4 HOLES Ø10
ON CRS Ø90

35

50

30

20

90

30

260

PRACTISE IN DRAWING LINES AND CIRCLES

6. Command: ELLIPSE: *Return*
    Axis endpoint 1: *pick*
    Axis endpoint 2: *pick*
    Other axis distance: *pick*
    Choose any sizes found to be convenient.
7. **Command: ELLIPSE:** *press Return*
    Center of ellipse: c *Return pick*
    Axis endpoint: *pick*
    Other axis distance: *pick*

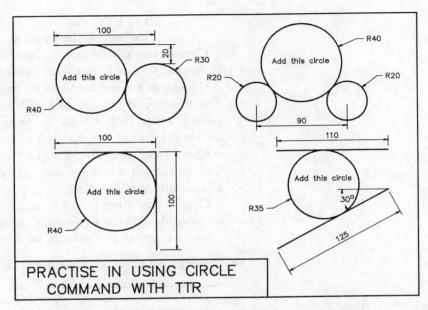

Fig. 2.19 Exercise 5

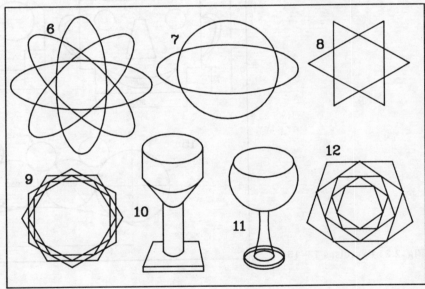

Fig. 2.20 Exercises 6–12

       Command: CIRCLE: *Return*
       Center point: *pick*
       Radius: *pick*
       Choose any sizes found to be convenient.

8. **Command: POLYGON:** *Return*
       Number of sides: 3 *press Return*
       Center of polygon: *pick*

I/C: i *Return*
    Radius of circle: *pick*
Choose any sizes found to be convenient.

9. Commands as in 8, but with number of sides: 6.
Choose any sizes found to be convenient.

10. The drawing is constructed with commands: **Ellipse**, **Arc (3-point)**, **Line**. Pick points as requested by prompts on the command line of the drawing editor.
Choose any sizes found to be convenient.

11. The outline of a wine glass can be drawn with commands: **Ellipse** and **Arc (3-point)**.
Choose any sizes found to be convenient.

12. Commands again as in 8 with number of sides: 5.
Choose any sizes found to be convenient.

The drawings for exercises 13–15 are given in Fig. 2.21.

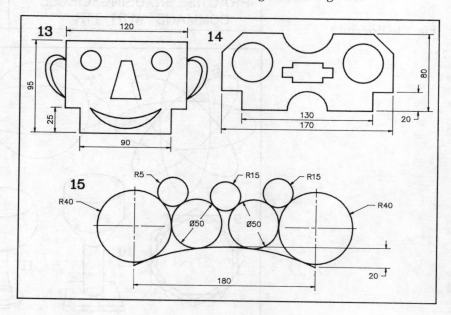

Fig. 2.21 Exercises 13–15

13. **Command: LINE:** draw lines by keying in relative coordinates at the command line prompts.
Command: CIRCLE: draw circles by picking estimated points.
Command: ARC: use **3-point** plus **CONTIN**ue for 'ears'.
    Use **3-point** for 'mouth'. Estimate sizes for 'ears': and 'mouth'.

14. Commands: **Line**, **Circle**, **Arc** (Centre, Start, End – C, S, E). Draw to given dimensions. Estimate sizes not given.

15. Work to the given dimensions. Commands: **ARC (3-point)**, **CIRCLE (TTR)**.
16. Several title blocks and types of notes seen on engineering drawings are shown in Fig. 2.22. The text consists of either *Complex* style or *Simplex* style fonts. The height of the text varies – some is 3, some 6, some 8, some 10 and some 15 high. Either copy the given title blocks or draw some to your own designs.

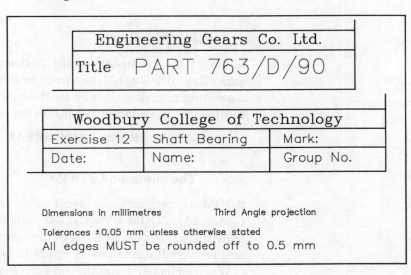

Fig. 2.22 Exercise 16

CHAPTER 3

Amending drawings

Introduction

Some of the commands most frequently required are those for amending drawings. The amendments may be for erasing or correcting mistakes or may be those which are part of a drawing routine. In this chapter the following commands are considered:

ZOOM, ERASE, TRIM, BREAK, CHANGE and **OFFSET**

The command ZOOM

ZOOM is probably the most often required of all AutoCAD's commands. **ZOOM** allows small parts of drawings to be accurately constructed, allows all parts of the screen to be minutely examined and enables the smallest of errors to be corrected or erased.

When selected from the on-screen menu, it will be seen that **ZOOM** is in the **DISPLAY** menu and has its own sub-menu as shown in Fig. 3.1. As with many other commands in AutoCAD, **ZOOM** can be selected from the on-screen menu, or from the pull-down menu **Display**, typed in as *zoom* at the command line or selected from a graphics tablet overlay.

The prompts in the **ZOOM** sub-menu which are of the most value are **All**, **Extents**, **Previous** and **Window**. Each can be called by typing in the initial letters *A*, *E*, *P* or *W* at the command line (or selecting from **ZOOM**'s on-screen sub-menu).

A (All): when **ZOOM A** is called, everything within the screen editor coordinate limits appears on screen. If any detail has been drawn outside the drawing editor limits, this will also appear in the screen drawing editor. It may be thought that this is not possible, but details outside the limits may appear either because of an earlier mistake or because the drawing limits have been changed.

E (Extents): when **ZOOM E** is called the screen drawing editor will

34

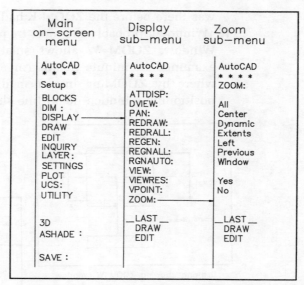

Fig. 3.1 The
DISPLAY–ZOOM on-screen
menu and sub-menus

change so that the drawing fits right up against the screen
drawing editor edges. Figure 3.2 gives two examples of a **ZOOM**
E call. The upper two drawings of Fig. 3.2 show a **ZOOM E** when
all of a drawing is within the set coordinate limits. The lower
two drawings of Fig. 3.2 show a **ZOOM E** when a detail has been
drawn outside the limits.

P (Previous): when **ZOOM P** is called what appears on screen is
what was there in the previous **ZOOM**. For example, if a **ZOOM**
E was showing, **ZOOM P** would set the screen back to show what

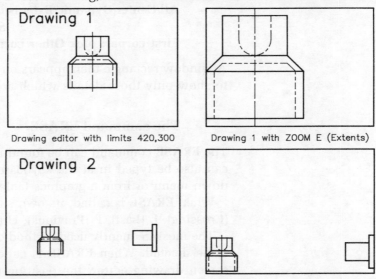

Fig. 3.2 Examples of **ZOOM**
Extents

Drawing editor with limits 420,300

Drawing 1 with ZOOM E (Extents)

Drawing with a detail outside limits

Drawing 2 with ZOOM E (Extents)

was there before the **ZOOM E** had been called.

W (Window): probably the most frequently used **ZOOM** prompt is Window. **ZOOM W** allows small areas of the screen to be examined in minute detail. An example is given in Fig. 3.3, where by **ZOOM**ing into a small **W**indow area, an error in positioning a hidden detail line shows up clearly.

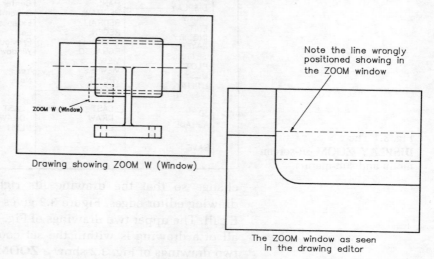

Drawing showing ZOOM W (Window)

The ZOOM window as seen in the drawing editor

Fig. 3.3 Example of **ZOOM** Window

The **Window** option of the **ZOOM** commands follows the procedure

Command: ZOOM
All/Center/Dynamic/Extents/Left/Previous/Window/
                               Scale(X)>: w *Keyboard Return*
First corner: *pick* **Other corner:** *pick*

A window rectangle then appears on screen and the screen changes to show only those details which are within the window.

The command ERASE

The **ERASE** command can be found in the **EDIT** on-screen menu. It can also be typed in at the keyboard, selected from the **Edit** pull-down menu or from a graphics tablet overlay.

When **ERASE** is called, its own sub-menu carries the prompts **C** (Crossing), **L** (Last), **P** (Previous), **U** (Undo) and **W** (Window).

The most frequently used method of erasure is to pick the objects to be deleted. When **ERASE** is called, a pick box appears in the screen drawing editor, the position of which is controlled by the pointing device. If an object is picked, it is highlighted by being changed to a broken line object. If *Return* is then pressed, the object so picked and highlighted disappears from the screen. See Fig. 3.4. The prompts are:

> **Command: ERASE**
> **Select object:** *pick* **1 selected, 1 found:**
> **Select object:** *Return*

and the object disappears from the screen.

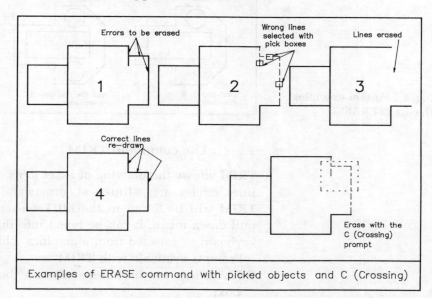

Fig. 3.4 Examples of the use of **ERASE**

Figure 3.4 also shows the effect of the **C** (Crossing) prompt with **ERASE**. All objects crossed by the crossing window box will be erased when *Return* is pressed. Figure 3.5 shows the effect of the **W** (Window) prompt of **ERASE**. It can be seen from Fig. 3.5 that the Window is used in a similar manner as when it is used with the **ZOOM** command, except that with **ERASE**, what is *completely* inside the box disappears when *Return* is pressed. Note the difference between **C** (Crossing) and **W** (Window) boxes. All objects crossed by the **C**rossing box disappear, whereas only objects completely enclosed by the **W**indows box disappear.

The **L** (Last) prompt of **ERASE** deletes the last object which has been drawn in the drawing editor.

OOPS: one important prompt associated with **ERASE** is **OOPS**. If an object has been erased by mistake, keying in or selecting **OOPS** causes the object deleted in error to reappear.

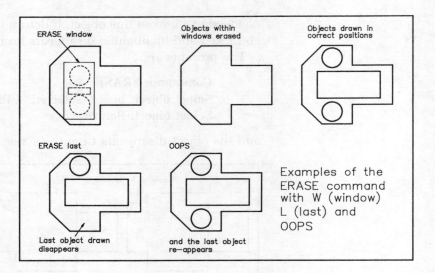

Fig. 3.5 Further examples of
the use of **ERASE**

The command TRIM

TRIM allows the drawing of exact joins of parts of objects such as
lines, circles, arcs, ellipses at corners and other intersection points.
TRIM will be found in the **EDIT** on-screen menu or in the **Edit**
pull-down menu; it can be typed into the command line from the
keyboard or selected from a graphics tablet overlay.

Prompts available with **TRIM** are:

C (Crossing): to trim objects meeting those crossed by a **C**rossing
box;

W (Window): to trim objects meeting those within a **w**indow box;

P (Previous): to highlight and so use again cutting edges of the last
called **TRIM** prompt;

A (Add): to add cutting edges after selecting other cutting edges by
picking, or by a **c**rossing or a **w**indows box.

TRIM functions as its name suggests. The command enables
objects to be **TRIM**med up to or between cutting edges which have
previously been highlighted by being selected from the **TRIM**
command. Figure 3.6 shows the sequence which is followed when
the command is called.

Figure 3.7 shows the method of producing a desired outline with
the aid of the command:

1. Construct the required outline with **line** and **circle**, without
    bothering too much about the positions of intersections
    between the objects;
2. Select line **cutting edges** to trim to by pointing the pick box;

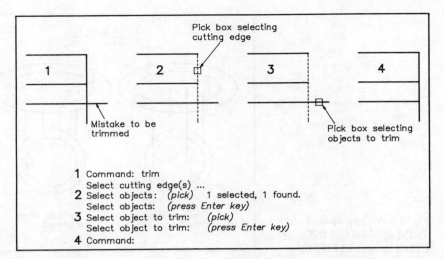

Fig. 3.6 Examples of the use of **TRIM**

3. Trim the parts of lines or circles to be deleted between the cutting edges;
4. Select the part-circle as a cutting edge;
5. Trim the two line ends up to the highlighted part-circle.

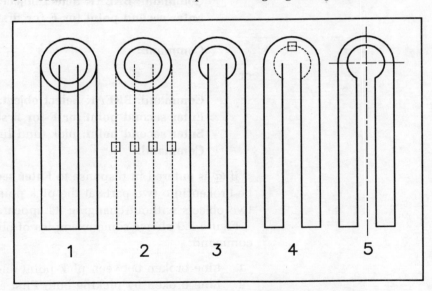

Fig. 3.7 A drawing showing how **TRIM** will produce accurate corner joins

Figure 3.8 is another example of **TRIM**ming between lines, circles and ellipses.

The command BREAK

BREAK is for breaking objects (lines, circles, etc.) into parts. **BREAK** can be selected from the **EDIT** on-screen menu, from the

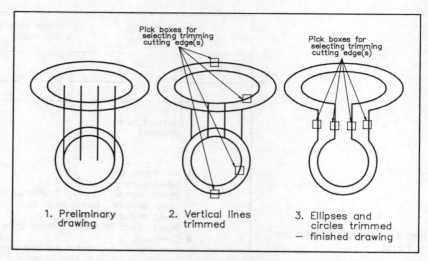

Fig. 3.8 An example of
TRIM applied to **LINE**s,
CIRCLEs and **ELLIPSE**s

Edit pull-down menu or typed in at the command line from the keyboard or selected from a graphics tablet overlay.

When **BREAK** is called the command line appears thus:

> **Command: BREAK Select object:** *pick*
> **Enter second point (or F for first point):** *pick (and line*
> *breaks)*
>
> **Command:**

or

> **Command: BREAK Select object:** *pick*
> **Enter second point (or F for first point):** f *Keyboard*
> **Enter second point:** *pick (and line breaks)*
> **Command:**

If @ is entered in response to **Enter second point:** the object will be broken into two parts at the pick point. The object will become two objects without changing its appearance.

Figure 3.9 shows some examples of objects being broken by this command:

1. Line broken between pick point and second point;
2. Line broken by picking both **F**irst and second points;
3. Circle broken between pick point and second point;
4. Notice that if the second point is picked clockwise from the first, it is the anticlockwise part of the circle that breaks;
5. A polygon broken between pick point and second point;
6. Notice that the anticlockwise rule also applies when a polygon is broken;

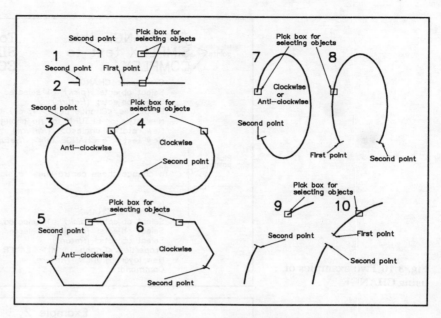

Fig. 3.9 Examples of how the command **BREAK** can be used

7.   An ellipse broken between pick and second points;
8.   An ellipse broken between First and second points;
9.   An arc broken between pick and second points;
10. An arc broken between First and second points.

The command CHANGE

If a mistake is made during a drawing session and it is not noticed until some time later, it may be possible to change the objects into their required form. Figure 3.10 gives examples of the changes which can be made: changing text styles and changing the linetype by layer.

Layers: This is possibly the most common form of change required. For information on layers see Chapter 4.

Other details: Other details such as colour and linetype can also be changed by keying in a *p* in response to the prompt

Properties/<Change point>:

and following the prompts from then on.

The command OFFSET

OFFSET is in the **DRAW** on-screen menu, or it may be typed in at the command line. The command allows objects to be drawn

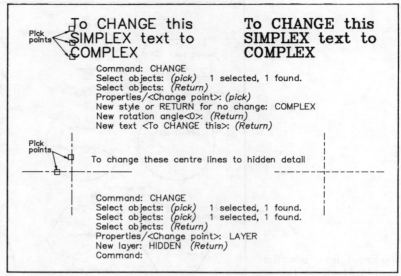

Fig. 3.10 Two examples of using **CHANGE**

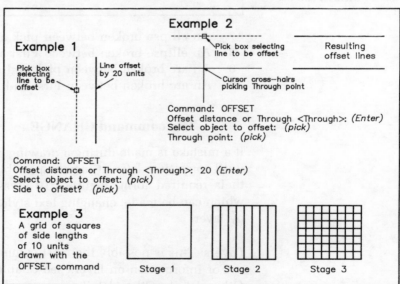

Fig. 3.11 Examples of lines **OFFSET** by stated unit lengths

parallel with each other, either at a stated distance typed at the command line in response to **Offset distance**, or at a distance from an original object picked with the pointing device. The command is easy to use, as can be seen with reference to Fig. 3.11.

Exercises

The following exercises are designed to give practice in the results of using commands **ERASE**, **TRIM**, **BREAK** and **OFFSET**. **ZOOM** will also be found to be of value when correcting small details in the finished drawings.

Note: These exercises will also emphasise the differences between the methods of drawing with instruments 'by hand' and drawing with the aid of CAD software.

Each of the Exercises 1–8 are shown in two parts. The drawings (a) describe original constructions and the drawings (b) the finished outlines.

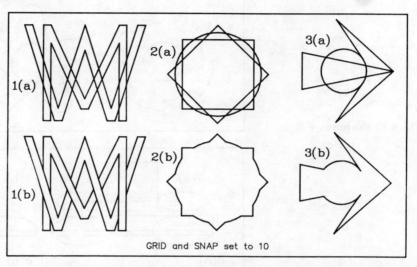

Fig. 3.12 Exercises 1–3

1.   Figure 3.12. Draw the monogram MW with the aid of **TRIM** to produce the exact outline.
2.   Figure 3.12. Draw the crossing circle and squares. Then with **TRIM** and **ERASE** complete the outline 2(b).
3.   Figure 3.12. Draw 3(a) with the aid of **LINE** and **CIRCLE**. Exact joins can be achieved with **OSNAP** together with **END**point and **TAN**gent. Then with **TRIM**, **ERASE** and perhaps **BREAK** produce the outline 3(b).
4–6.   Draw each of the three locking tab washers of Fig. 3.13, by first drawing the constructions 4(a), 4(b) and 4(c), then completing the outlines with the aid of **TRIM**, **BREAK** and **ERASE**.
7.   Figure 3.14. Draw the outline of a pedestal given by 7(b). Commence with lines and ellipses as in 7(a) and then **TRIM** intersections to produce the required outline.
8.   Figure 3.14. Draw the grid of lines 8(a). Then **TRIM** unwanted parts of lines to give 8(b).
9.   With **OFFSET** and **TRIM** draw a maze similar to that given in Fig. 3.15.

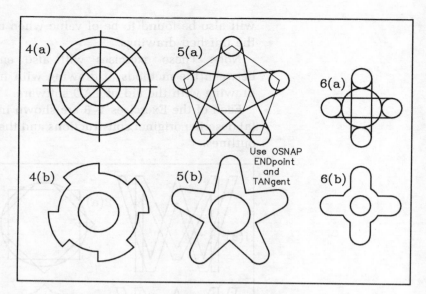

Fig. 3.13 Exercises 4—6

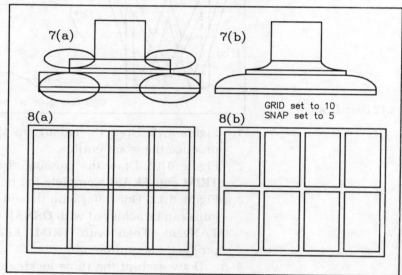

Fig. 3.14 Exercises 7 and 8

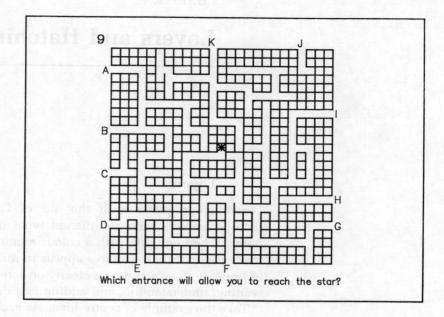

Fig. 3.15 Exercise 9

CHAPTER 4

Layers and Hatching

Layers

Drawings produced with the aid of CAD software frequently
include features such as different types of lines, dimensions and
notes. When working with a colour monitor, drawing on screen is
made easier if these features appear in different colours. Each type
of line, say, then stands out clearly on screen. This makes for easier
reading, understanding and adding to a drawing.

Take the example of centre lines. As each group of centre lines is
added to a drawing on screen, the colour and the spacings between
parts of the lines can be changed by calling up the command
linetype (from the **SETTINGS** on-screen menu) and following the
prompts which then appear. Then when reverting back to outline
lines, the command **linetype** must be selected again and the type of
line changed back.

A quicker (and easier) method of changing is to place each type
of line and features such as notes (text) and dimensions on to
LAYERs. Then when a **layer** is selected – say the layer for centre
lines – lines drawn when that layer is **current** will appear as centre
lines in a chosen colour.

Note: Although the full advantages of drawing on layers are
gained with a colour monitor, the methods of drawing features such
as different linetypes on separate layers still apply when a
monochrome screen is fitted at the workstation.

CAD drawing can include as many layers as the draughtsman
thinks fit. Each layer can be regarded as one of a set of tracings
which fit perfectly over a base drawing (on layer 0). As with actual
tracings a sheet (layer) can be removed when necessary. So with
AutoCAD layers. They can be turned **OFF** (not seen) or **ON** (seen)
as required. Figure 4.1 shows a CAD drawing of a simple
engineering assembly which has been constructed on layers, each
of a different colour. This drawing was produced on six layers:

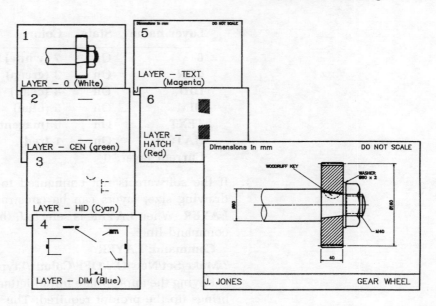

Fig. 4.1 A drawing
constructed on six layers

Layer 0	outlines — white
Layer CEN	centre lines — green
Layer HID	hidden detail lines — cyan
Layer DIM	dimensions — blue
Layer TEXT	all text — magenta
Layer HATCH	hatch lines — red

Notes

1. When the drawing editor first appears for a new drawing, the current layer will be layer 0;
2. Layers can be given any name. The layers of Fig. 4.1 could have been named 0 and 1–5; or 0, then C (for centre), H (for hidden) and so on; or any other system a draughtsman thinks suitable;
3. AutoCAD is usually configured so that when a new drawing is started by selecting:

1. Begin a NEW drawing

from the **Main menu** (see p. 2), a specific sheet size with layers for the type of drawing usually constructed at the workstation will appear on screen. If so, the layers that have been pre-set can be seen by typing or selecting **layer** as a command, typing ?, and pressing *Return* twice. A list will then appear on screen such as:

Layer name	State	Color	Linetype
0	On	7 (white)	CONTINUOUS
CEN	On	3 (green)	CENTER
HID	On	4 (cyan)	HIDDEN
DIM	On	5 (blue)	CONTINUOUS
TEXT	On	6 (magenta)	CONTINUOUS
HATCH	On	1 (red)	CONTINUOUS

Current layer: 0

4. If the software is not configured to produce a specific sheet drawing size, layers can be constructed under the command **LAYER**. When **LAYER** is selected, the following appears at the command line:

    Command: LAYER
    ?/Make/Set/New/ON/OFF/Colour/Ltype/Freeze/Thaw:

    Keying the appropriate initial letter, or the words *ON* or *OFF*, brings up the prompt required. The prompts are:

    Make – makes a new layer, which then becomes the current layer;

    Set – sets the current layer;

    New – makes a new layer, but it does not become the current layer;

    ON – turns a layer **on**;

    OFF – turns a layer **off**;

    Freeze – the layer is **off** when the drawing regenerates;

    Thaw – thaws a frozen layer.

5. A frozen layer cannot be turned **ON**. It must be first thawed.

6. Details of the layers in a drawing can also be seen by selecting **Modify layer** . . . from the **Settings** pull-down menu. A dialogue box such as that shown in Fig. 4.2 then appears in the centre of the screen drawing area. The method of selection from this dialogue box is by pointing and picking with the pointer device. If one of the ticks is pointed at, it will change to a blank box when picked, and vice versa. When a description is pointed at, a new description can be typed in or selected from further dialogue boxes associated with the picked name;

7. The characters * ? \ and / cannot be included in the name of a layer.

Hatching

If the **Draw** pull-down menu is selected from the status line, it will be seen that one selection from the **Draw** menu is **Hatch** . . . .

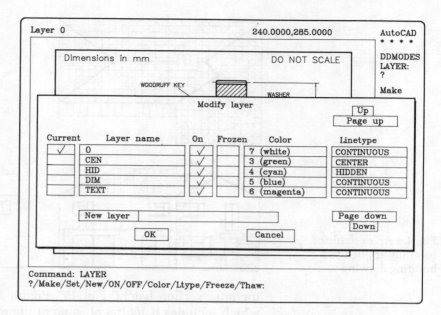

Fig. 4.2 The pull-down dialogue box for controlling layers

Pointing and picking **Hatch** . . . results in a dialogue box appearing mid-screen, in which a number of hatch patterns are shown. There are more than one dialogue boxes associated with this command. If **Next** is selected from the first Hatch dialogue box, a second will appear and a third from the second. This all gives a number of different hatch patterns. Each pattern can be changed as to size and angle of rotation when using the **HATCH** command from the command line. Figures 4.3 and 4.4 are drawings involving hatching from AutoCAD. Figure 4.3 is a simple engineering drawing which

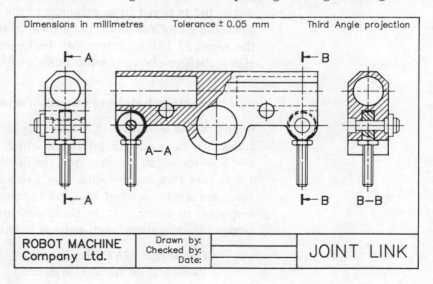

Fig. 4.3 An example of hatching in sectional views

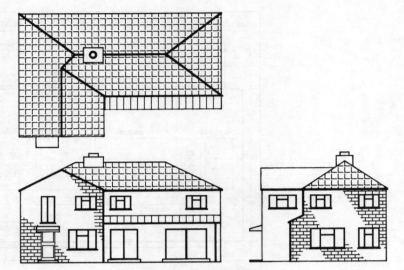

Fig. 4.4 An example of hatching applied to a building drawing

includes section hatching at 45°. Figure 4.4 is a building drawing which includes hatching of some of the roof areas and parts of the walls.

When the command **HATCH** is called, the command line of the drawing editor shows

>**Command: HATCH**
>**Pattern (? or name/U,style):**

Each hatch pattern which appears when **Hatch** ... is selected from the **Draw** pull-down menu is given a name – e.g. the name of the wall hatch pattern of Fig. 4.4 is *brick*, the roof tile pattern is *angle*. If ? is keyed in in response to the **HATCH** prompts, a list of available AutoCAD hatch patterns appears on screen. The name of the required hatch pattern can be keyed in rather than from the Hatch dialogue box from the pull-down menu, if wished.

Section hatching in engineering drawings

Figure 4.5 is a third angle orthographic drawing of a lathe lead screw. To demonstrate problems which can arise when hatching and how these can be overcome, the hatching of section A–A of Fig. 4.5 is taken as an example. The hatching lines in this sectional view are at 45° spaced at 4 units apart. The following are the responses to prompts at the command line of the drawing editor to achieve the required hatch pattern in this example.

>**Command: HATCH**
>**Pattern (? or name/U,style):** u   *Keyboard Return*

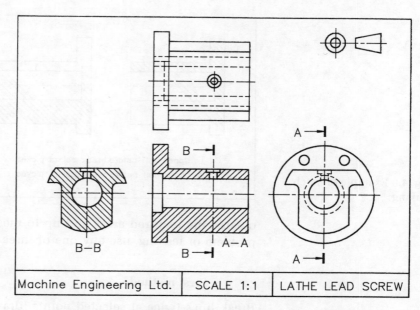

Machine Engineering Ltd. | SCALE 1:1 | LATHE LEAD SCREW

Fig. 4.5 An engineering drawing with hatched sectional views

Angle for crosshatch lines <0<: 45 *Keyboard Return*
Spacing between lines <1.0000>: 4 *Keyboard Return*
Double hatch area? <N>: *Return*
Select objects: *and a pick box appears Pick each object in turn Return*
Command:

As each object (line, arc, circle, etc.) is picked, the object is highlighted by changing to a dotted appearance. When the final object surrounding the area to be hatched has been picked and *Return* pressed, the area is automatically filled with the required hatch pattern.

Leaking

When an object surrounding an area to be hatched is selected, the whole of that object is regarded by AutoCAD as the hatch boundary. Unless precautions are taken when defining hatch boundaries, *leaking* of the hatching can occur. This problem is shown in Fig. 4.6.

In Fig. 4.6, the outlines of section A–A were drawn without regard to the fact that parts of the drawing were to be hatched. When each object (line) surrounding the hatched areas had been selected, the hatching appeared as shown. AutoCAD regarded the left-hand and right-hand lines of the outline for example as hatching boundaries, with the result that the hatching leaked

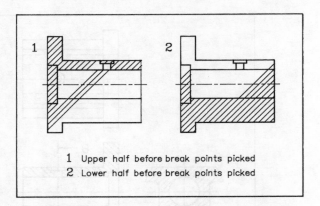

1 Upper half before break points picked
2 Lower half before break points picked

Fig. 4.6 Example of hatch
leaking

outside the required areas and up to these lines. To overcome the
problem of leaking, use any one of three methods.

First method

Break lines twice at selected points (drawing 1 of Fig. 4.7). Select
the **BREAK** command:

Command: BREAK
Select object: *pick*
Enter second point (or F for first point): f *Keyboard Return*
Enter first point: *pick*
Enter second point: *pick same point*
Command:

and the object is broken at the twice picked point. The object is
now in two parts as if drawn as two separate objects. Or

Select object: *pick at required break point*
Enter second point (or F for first point): @ *Keyboard
Return*
Command:

and the object is broken into parts at the picked point.

Second method

This method employs a separate layer for drawing hatch area
outline (Fig. 4.8) in which this layer is named H. The procedure
would follow a routine such as:

1. Draw the full sectional view outline on layer 0;
2. Make a new layer H (or any other suitable name) – preferably

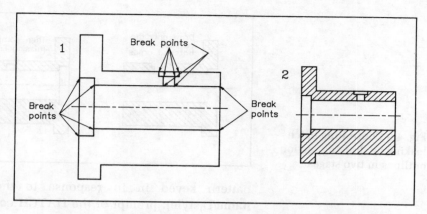

Fig. 4.7 How breaking join of lines prevents hatch leaking

with a colour different from either layer 0 or layer HATCH;

3. Draw separate outlines on layer H of the two areas of section A–A which is to be filled with hatching lines;

4. Set layer HATCH. Hatch the areas drawn on layer H while in layer HATCH;

5. Turn layer H **OFF**. This leaves the outline on layer 0, with hatched areas correctly filled.

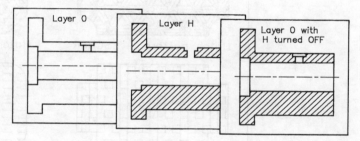

Fig. 4.8 Controlling hatch leaking by drawing sectional view outlines on a separate layer

Third method

Draw only the outlines of areas to be hatched on layer 0 (Fig. 4.9). Set layer HATCH and hatch these areas. Now set layer 0 and fill in those parts of the outline which had not been drawn previously.

The choice is the draughtsman's. The three methods defined above may appear somewhat complex. In fact they are quite simple to follow when working in AutoCAD. The time taken to explain them is much greater than the time taken to use them.

Examples

Figure 4.10 gives examples of areas hatched with selected AutoCAD hatch patterns. Such patterns may be selected from **Hatch** ... from the **Draw** pull-down menu or the name of the

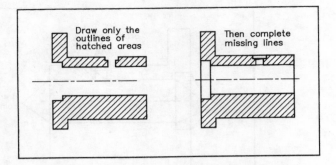

Fig. 4.9 Controlling hatch
leaking by drawing section
outlines in two stages

pattern keyed in in response to the prompt **Pattern (? or name/U,style):** prompt of the **HATCH** command. The reader might wish to practise in the use of hatch patterns such as are shown in this illustration.

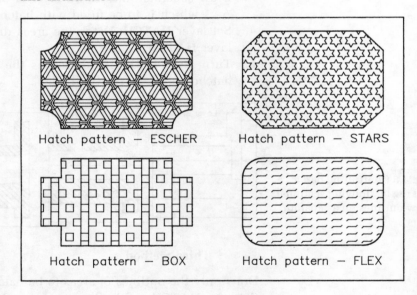

Fig. 4.10 Examples of
AutoCAD hatch patterns

Exercises

Exercises 1–4 are based on the drawings of Fig. 4.11.

1. With commands **arc**, **line**, **circle**, **polygon**, **trim**, **text** and **hatch**, draw the given items of graphics.
2. Using commands **line**, **offset**, **trim** and **hatch**, draw a monogram involving your own initials.
3. Draw the given arrow. Commands – **line**, **arc**, **hatch**.
4. Draw two quadrilaterals, one inside the other. Then hatch the space between with the AutoCAD hatch pattern EARTH.

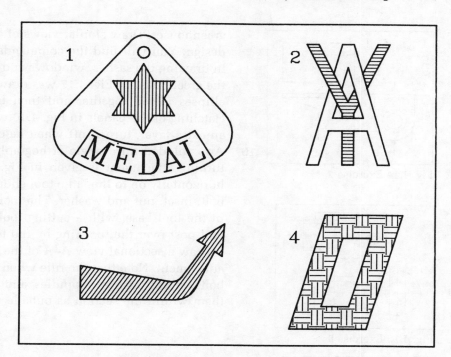

Fig. 4.11 Exercises 1–4

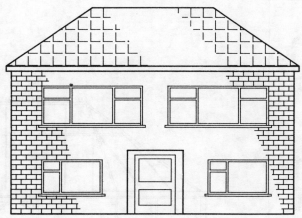

Fig. 4.12 Exercise 5

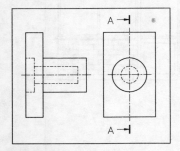

Fig. 4.13 Exercise 6

5. Figure 4.12. A front view of a two-storey house is shown. Draw a similar view of a house. The commands **offset** and **trim** will be of value in accurately drawing the window and door frames. The hatching of the walls and roof will require an extra layer, which must be turned **OFF** after use.

6. Figure 4.13. Draw and section hatch section A–A.

7. Figure 4.14. Draw and section hatch section C–C.

8. Figure 4.15. Draw and section hatch section B–B.

9. Figures 4.16 and 4.17 show orthographic views of two

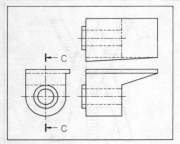

Fig. 4.14 Exercise 7

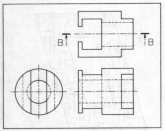

Fig. 4.15 Exercise 8

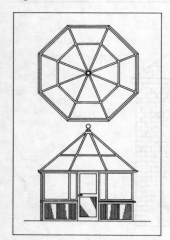

Fig. 4.16 Example for
Exercise 9

Fig. 4.17 Example for
Exercise 9

greenhouses. Draw similar views of a greenhouse of your own design. You will find the commands **offset** and **trim** of value in drawing the sashes, windows and door frames. The ridge of the greenhouse of Fig. 4.17 was drawn from a series of similar ellipses joined together and then trimmed to form a ridge. Hatching of the panels in Fig. 4.16 was achieved by including an extra layer, turned **off** when hatching was completed.

10. An exploded third angle orthographic projection of a sphere turning attachment is given in Fig. 4.18. The Tool base fits horizontally on to the lathe tool slide and is bolted to it by the bolt, inset, nut and washer. The tool post fits through the slot in the tool base, with a cutting tool (not shown) held in the tool post over the tool ring by the tool retaining bolt.

Draw a sectional view A–A of the assembled sphere turning attachment. Note that the rule when drawing sections through bolts, nuts, washers, spindles and similar parts is to draw them within the section as outside views.

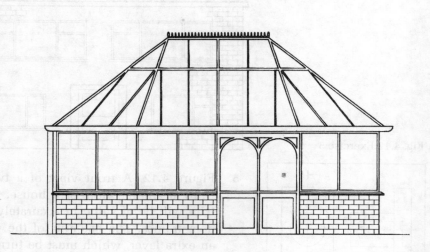

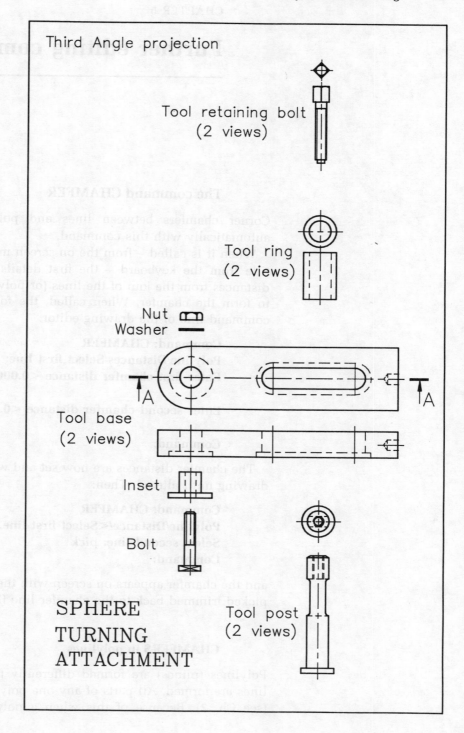

Third Angle projection

Tool retaining bolt
(2 views)

Tool ring
(2 views)

Nut
Washer

Tool base
(2 views)

Inset

Bolt

SPHERE
TURNING
ATTACHMENT

Tool post
(2 views)

A

A

Fig. 4.18 Exercise 10

CHAPTER 5

Further editing commands

The command CHAMFER

Corner chamfers between lines and polylines can be drawn automatically with this command.

When it is called – from the on-screen menu or by keying in its title from the keyboard – the first details to be entered are the distances from the join of the lines (or polylines) that are required to form the chamfer. When called, the following appears at the command line of the drawing editor:

Command: CHAMFER
Polyline/Distances/Select first line: d *Keyboard Return*
Enter first chamfer distance <0.0000>: 20 *Keyboard*
Return
Enter second chamfer distance <0.0000>: 30 *Keyboard*
Return
Command:

The chamfer distances are now set and will be retained with the drawing until altered. Then:

Command: CHAMFER
Polyline/Distance/<Select first line>: *pick*
Select second line: *pick*
Command:

and the chamfer appears on screen with the lines which have been picked trimmed back to the chamfer line (Fig. 5.1).

CHAMFERS in polylines

Polylines (plines) are formed differently from the way in which lines are formed. All parts of any one polyline act as a single unit (see Ch. 2). Because of this when a polyline is chamfered, the

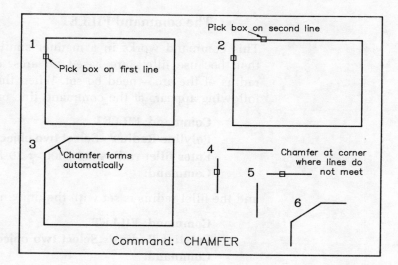

Fig. 5.1 Stages in producing
a **CHAMFER** in lines

whole pline automatically chamfers at every corner. Three examples
are given in Fig. 5.2. When chamfering polylines, the prompt

Polyline/Distance/<Select first line>:

must be answered with a p. Otherwise the software ignores the
request to chamfer the polyline.

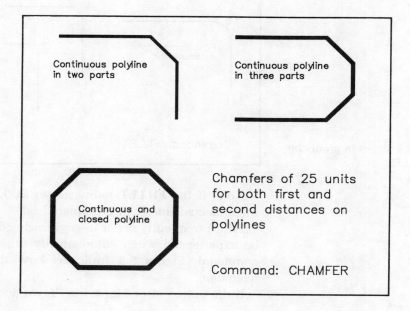

Fig. 5.2 Stages in producing
a **CHAMFER** in plines

The command FILLET

This command works in a manner similar to **CHAMFER**, except that, because fillets are based on arcs, only one distance – the radius of the arc – need be set. When the command is called the following appears at the command line of the drawing editor:

> **Command: FILLET**
> **Polyline/Radius/<Select two objects>:** r *Keyboard Return*
> **Enter fillet radius <0.0000>:** 20 *Keyboard Return*
> **Command:**

and the fillet radius is set with the drawing until it is altered. Then

> **Command: FILLET**
> **Polyline/Radius/<Select two objects>:** *pick both objects*
> **Command:**

and the fillet appears on screen with the two objects trimmed back to the fillet arc (Fig. 5.3).

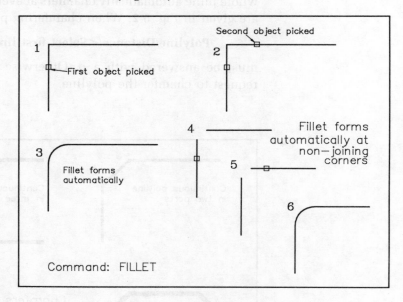

Fig. 5.3 Stages in producing a **FILLET**

Note: If the **FILLET** radius is set at 0, two intersecting or two unconnected lines can be 'squared off'.

Fillets frequently occur in engineering drawings. Difficulties may be experienced when automatically drawing them from the **fillet** command. Figure 5.3 indicates how these difficulties may be overcome.

If the outline 1 of Fig. 5.4 is drawn and then the required fillets added, the fillets appear as in drawing 2. As this is not what is required, either the original outline needs to be drawn as in drawing 3 before the fillets are added, or as in drawing 6. In both cases the shoulder line of the spindle will have to be completed after the fillets have been added.

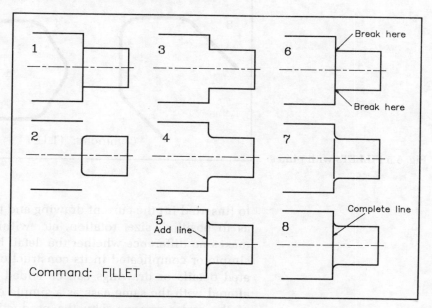

Fig. 5.4 Overcoming problems when using **FILLET**

FILLETs in polylines

When adding fillets to polylines, the same problem arises as when chamfering polylines. The whole of the pline acts as a single unit. The results of fillets being added to plines are indicated in Fig. 5.5. As with chamfers, the prompt

Polyline/Radius/<Select two objects>:

must be answered with a *p Return* before the fillets will appear on plines.

Never draw the same thing twice

When drawing with the aid of CAD software, the operator should aim at never having to draw the same thing twice. If taken in its broadest sense, this aim applies not only to the current drawing, but also to all the drawings which can be produced at a workstation. When drawing with AutoCAD, any object or detail in a drawing can be moved, copied, mirrored, rotated, scaled or stretched. In addition, details from previous drawings can be added

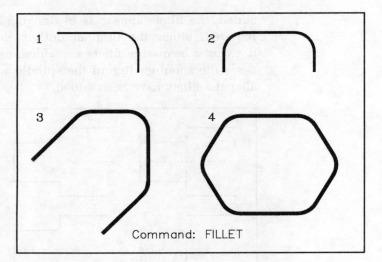

Command: FILLET

Fig. 5.5 **FILLET**s with plines

to (inserted in) the current drawing and the insertion can be altered as to position, size, rotation, etc. within the current drawing. It makes no difference whether the detail being added or amended is simple or complicated in its construction. Even the most complicated details or drawings can be added to the current drawing or altered with the same ease as a simple one. Such facilities are one of the major reasons why the production of drawing with CAD software takes far less time than when drawing by hand. The rule to follow is:

Never draw the same thing twice

and try to take advantage of all the facilities in AutoCAD to achieve the aim of observing the rule.

Among others, there are seven principal command systems in AutoCAD, which are designed to ensure this rule can be followed. Later in this book we shall come across others. These seven command systems are:

ARRAY, **COPY**, **MIRROR**, **MOVE**, **ROTATE**, **SCALE** and **STRETCH**

Each of the commands in this series has a set of prompts with similar features.

Common details with this group of seven commands

When any of the commands in this group are called, the prompt

Select objects:

will appear at the command line. The seven commands have a number of common responses to this prompt. These are:

Window (w) – requires the picking of the two corners of a window frame enclosing *all* the objects to be operated on by the command;

Crossing (c) – also requires two corners of a window crossing the objects to be operated on by the command;

Last (l) – selects the last object to be operated on by the command;

Previous (p) – selects the objects previously selected;

Remove (r) – removes objects from those already selected, but only when the selection has been completed;

Add (a) – adds a further object to those already selected;

Undo (u) – undoes the last object selected immediately following its selection.

The two responses **U**ndo and **R**emove allow correction when the wrong object(s) have been chosen. Remove is only effective after all objects have been selected. Note that an individual object from within a window can be removed if necessary. Undo must be used immediately an object has been selected if it has been chosen by mistake.

Note: When **STRETCH** has been chosen, a **W**indow (**w**) (usually a **C**rossing window (**c**)), must be the selection response.

When the response to

Select objects:

is *w* or *c*, **1 selected, 1 found.** becomes e.g. **4 selected, 4 found.**, depending upon the number of objects within the selection box. If the window encloses previously selected objects, a response such as **4 found, (2 duplicate).** might be seen.

Select objects: appears a second time after each object or group of objects has been selected. The **Select objects:** response only changes to another prompt when *Return* has been pressed.

The commands COPY and MOVE

A typical example of one of this set of seven commands is **COPY**. When this is called, the following appears at the command line:

Command: COPY
Select objects: *pick* 1 selected, 1 found.
Select objects: *Return*

<**Base point or displacement**>/**Multiple:** *pick* **Second point**
of displacement: *pick*

Command:

or

Command: COPY
Select objects: w *(keyboard) Return*
First corner: *pick* **Other corner:** *pick* **4 found.**
Select objects: *Return*
<**Base point or displacement**>/**Multiple:** *pick* **Second point**
of displacement: *pick*
Command:

Two examples of the **COPY** command in use are given in Fig. 5.6.
The objects were placed in a window for copying and in each
example multiple copies were requested.

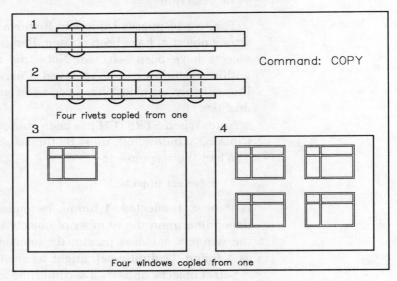

Fig. 5.6 Example of the use
of **COPY**

COPY can be used to produce multiple pattern drawings quickly.
Figure 5.7 is an example.

The **MOVE** command is similar to the **COPY** command except
that no **M**ultiple move is possible.

Two examples of objects that have been **MOVE**d are given in Fig.
5.8. In both examples the objects were placed in a window before
being **move**d. **MOVE** is of particular value when completing a
drawing to obtain the best possible layout. Each and every feature
of a drawing can be **MOVE**d to a new position in order to improve
the layout of the whole drawing.

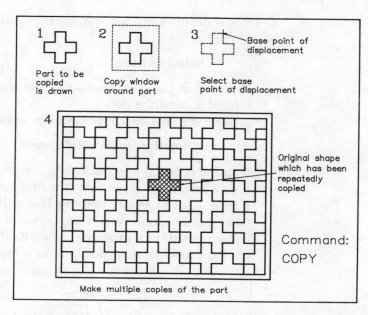

Fig. 5.7 An example of
multiple **COPY**ing

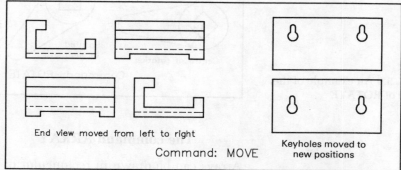

Fig. 5.8 An example of the
use of **MOVE**

The command ROTATE

Figure 5.9 is an example of a detail in a drawing which has been
rotated. The prompts appearing at the command line of the
drawing editor are

> **Command: ROTATE**
> **Select objects:** *pick*
> **Select objects:** *Return*
> **Base point:** *pick*
> **<Rotation angle>/Reference:** 45 *Keyboard Return*
> **Command:**

Note: The **Base point:** is the centre about which rotation takes
place.

The detail in Fig. 5.9 was placed within a window and when the prompt

Select objects:

appeared at the command line, a **w** was keyed in and a window formed around the detail.

Note: If **r** (**R**eference) is keyed in answer to the prompt

<Rotation angle>/Reference:

then the object(s) selected can be *dragged* around the base point as if on a line. If **r** is given as 0°, the drag line will be horizontal on the screen. If given as 90°, the drag line will be vertical on the screen. Other angle numbers can be keyed in if required. If objects are being rotated on a drag line, when *Return* is pressed, the object(s) are then fixed in their position on screen.

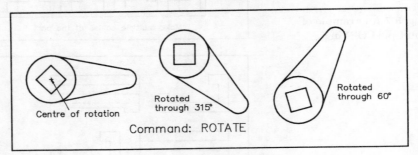

Fig. 5.9 An example of the use of **ROTATE**

The command ARRAY

Arrays can be drawn in *rectangular* or *polar* form. If rectangular, a detail in a drawing can be copied in a number of rows (horizontally) and a number of columns (vertically). If polar, the detail can be copied in a circular form around a central (base) point. The number of rows and columns or the number of copies in a polar array is keyed in at the appropriate responses when the command **ARRAY** is called.

Rectangular ARRAY

When **ARRAY** is called, the command line appears as follows:

Command: ARRAY
Select objects: *pick*
Select objects: *Return*
Rectangular or Polar array (R/P): r *Keyboard Return*

Number of rows (——) <1>: 4 *Keyboard Return*
Number of columns (| | |) <1>: 3 *Keyboard Return*
Unit cell or distance between rows (——): 40 *Return*
Distance between columns (| |): 30 *Return*
Command:

Note: Distances between rows and columns are based upon the centre point of the selected object(s).

If rows are required below the selected object(s) **Distance between rows:** must be answered with a negative (-ve) number. If columns are required to the left of the selected object(s), **Distance between columns:** must be answered with a negative (-ve) number.

Polar ARRAY

If a polar array is required a *p* is keyed in answer to **(R/P)** and the sequence becomes

Rectangular or Polar array (R/P): p *Keyboard Return*
Center of array: *pick*
Number of items: 15 *Keyboard Return*
Angle to fill (+=ccw, −=cw) <360>: *Return*
Rotate objects as they are copied? <Y< *Return*
Command:

Examples of polar and rectangular arrays are given in Fig. 5.10.

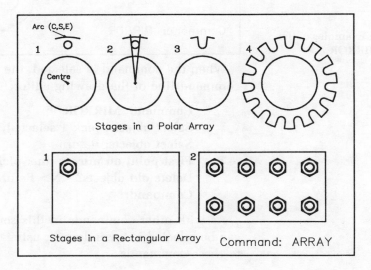

Fig. 5.10 Examples of Polar and Rectangular **ARRAY**s

The command MIRROR

When details in a drawing are symmetrical about a line or about lines, only part of the detail need be drawn. Other parts can then be **MIRROR**ed about the line(s) of symmetry. This command is also of value if a detail in a drawing needs to be reversed in direction, say from facing left to facing right or facing up instead of facing down. This can be achieved by answering Y to the prompt **Delete old objects?** <**N**>: during the sequence of prompts initiated when the command is called.

Figure 5.11 shows two examples of drawings completed by using **MIRROR**. Drawings 1 and 2 of Fig. 5.11 show how a mirror image is copied around a single line of symmetry. Drawings 3, 4 and 5 of Fig. 5.11 show how only a quarter of a symmetrical detail need be drawn, the remainder being copied by **MIRROR**ing around two lines of symmetry.

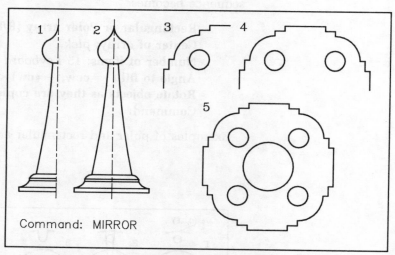

Command: MIRROR

Fig. 5.11 Examples of the use of **MIRROR**

When the command is selected, the following will appear at the command line of the drawing editor:

> **Command: MIRROR**
> **Select objects:** *pick* **1 selected, 1 found.**
> **Select objects:** *Return*
> **First point on mirror line:** *pick* **Second point:** *pick*
> **Delete old objects?** <**N**> *Return (or Y if deletion required)*
> **Command:**

As with other commands in this set, the objects to be mirrored can be selected in a window, or using the other responses common to these commands.

The commands SCALE and STRETCH

With the aid of these two command structures, details in drawings can be enlarged or reduced in size or can be stretched in any direction. Figure 5.12 shows how a drawing of a bolt can be **SCALE**d and/or **STRETCH**ed to produce a number of drawings of bolts of different lengths and diameters, without having to redraw the bolt each time.

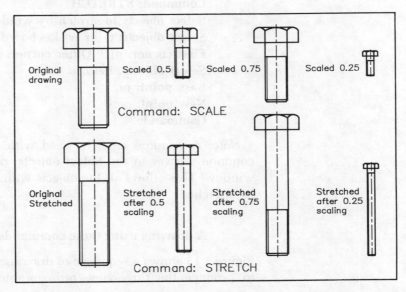

Fig. 5.12 **SCALE** and **STRETCH** applied to drawings of bolts

The command line sequence of prompts for both **SCALE** and **STRETCH** are given below. Note that the response *w* (window) or *c* (crossing) can be given when the **Select objects:** prompt appears.

Command: SCALE
Select objects: *pick* **1 selected, 1 found**
Select objects: *Return*
Base point: *pick*
<Scale factor>/Reference: 2 *Return*
Command:

Note: The **Scale factor:** can be a whole or a decimal number, smaller or greater than 1. A scale factor less than 1 reduces the object(s) in size; one greater than 1 increases the size of the object(s).

If r is keyed in response to the

<Scale factor>/Reference:

prompt, a further prompt appears:

Reference length <1>:

If a figure is keyed in another prompt appears:

New length:.

The figures given in response to these two prompts determine the ratio of the scale – e.g. 3:5, 8:5 and so on.

> **Command: STRETCH**
> **Select objects to stretch by window . . .**
> **Select objects:** c (or w) *Keyboard Return*
> **First corner:** *pick* **Other corner:** *pick*
> **Select objects:** *Return*
> **Base point:** *pick*
> **New point:** *pick*
> **Command:**

Note: A window must be used with this command. The most common answer to the **Select objects:** prompt is c for a Crossing window. This allows all the objects within the Crossing window to be stretched.

A drawing using these commands

Figure 5.13 shows a sequence of drawings which could be followed to produce the three-view orthographic projection of a spindle

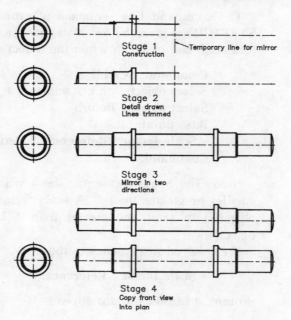

Stage 1
Construction   Temporary line for mirror

Stage 2
Detail drawn
Lines trimmed

Stage 3
Mirror in two
directions

Stage 4
Copy front view
into plan

Fig. 5.13 Stages in producing
an AutoCAD drawing

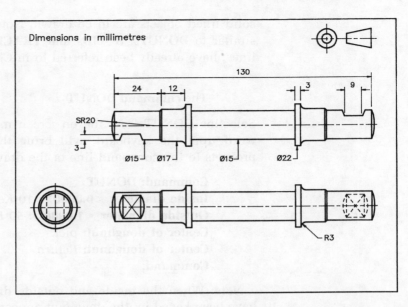

Fig. 5.14 The finished
drawing

given in Fig. 5.14. This sequence involves using some of the
commands outlined in this chapter.

Figure 5.13 Stage 1. First draw (on layer CEN) the centre lines for
both the end view and the front view.

Add a central vertical line around which the left-hand part of
the front view can be mirrored. This vertical centre line will be
erased later. Set layer 0 and draw the end view — a series of
circles based on the crossing centre lines.

From these circles project lines of the outline of a quarter of
the front view. Use the relative coordinates method to ensure
these lines are correctly positioned.

Stage 2. Complete the quarter view — **chamfer, fillet, arc** and **trim**
unnecessary lines.

Stage 3. **Mirror** the quarter view to right and below. **Erase** the
vertical centre line around which the right-hand half of the front
view has been mirrored.

Stage 4. **Copy** the front view to give the third (plan) view.

Figure 5.14. Add the spindle flats, hidden detail, text, a margin and
the dimensions. Note that methods of adding dimensions will be
dealt with later (Ch. 7).

Commands DONUT, SOLID and TRACE

Three commands which are not part of the set of seven outlined
above can now be explained. These three commands are used when

solid filled objects are to be drawn. Note that **PLINE**s, which are similar to **DONUT**s, **SOLID**s and **TRACE**s, in that they are filled lines,* have already been referred to in Chapter 2.

The command DONUT

Selecting **DONUT** from the on-screen menu, or by keying in the word from the keyboard, will bring the following sequence of prompts to the command line of the drawing editor:

> **Command: DONUT**
> **Inside diameter <0.0000>:** 10 *Keyboard Return*
> **Outside diameter <1.0000>:** 50 *Keyboard Return*
> **Center of doughnut:** *pick*
> **Center of doughnut:** *Return*
> **Command:**

Note: When the inside and outside diameters of the doughnut have been keyed in, the doughnut appears on screen to be dragged into position by moving the pointing device. When the centre of the doughnut has been picked, the doughnut is then fixed in position on the screen and a new centre can be picked without again selecting the command. The prompt **Center of doughnut:** repeats after each doughnut has been placed in position on the screen.

Note: A doughnut can be only **trim**med against a line which has been drawn through its centre – **trim**ming to such a line results in half a doughnut.

Doughnuts without a centre hole can be drawn by answering the **Inside diameter <0.0000>:** prompt either by pressing *Return* or with a 0 if the default value at the prompt is not **<0.0000>**. The solid filled circle which results from this can be used in details such as electronic circuit drawing where the small filled doughnuts can be placed at all joining conductor points. Examples of doughnuts are given in Fig. 5.15.

The command SOLID

Figure 5.15 also includes a *filled* rectangle which has been drawn by using the **SOLID** command.

When areas of outlines are to be filled, AutoCAD performs the **FILL** operation as if the area of the outline is a series of adjacent triangles. This entails the picking of corners in answer to responses within the command structure as shown in the filled rectangle of Fig. 5.15.

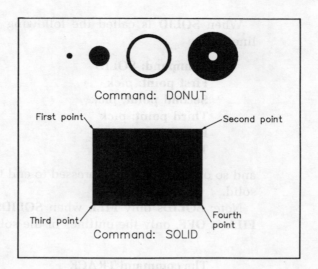

Fig. 5.15 Examples of the use of **DONUT** and **SOLID**

After picking two points along one side of the rectangle, the third pick point is taken *diagonally* opposite the second, with the fourth pick point diagonally opposite the first. In this way a rectangle is *filled* as if it were two adjacent triangles. This method of picking corners in order to fill an outline is further extended to more complicated outlines in Fig. 5.16. In each of the three *filled* outlines in this illustration, the order of picking is shown by a number sequence in each case.

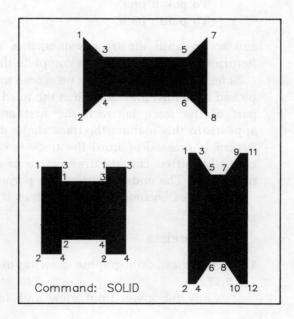

Fig. 5.16 Examples of the order of picking when **SOLID** is called

When **SOLID** is called the following appears at the command line:

> **Command: SOLID**
> **First point:** *pick*
> **Second point:** *pick*
> **Third point:** *pick*
> **Fourth point:** *pick*
> **Third point:** *pick*

and so on until *Return* is pressed to end the session of drawing the solid.

Note: **SOLID**s only **FILL** when **SOLIDS FILL** is **ON**. If **SOLIDS FILL** is **OFF**, only the outlines of the solid appears on screen.

The command TRACE

A **TRACE** is a line similar to a **pline**, except that a **trace** can only be in the form of a straight line. **Trace** arcs and other shapes are not possible. **Trace**s cannot be chamfered or filleted. **Trace**s can be altered with **BREAK** but not with **TRIM**.

When **TRACE** is called the following appears:

> **Command: TRACE**
> **Trace width <0.5000>:** 10 *Keyboard Return*
> **From point:** *pick*
> **To point:** *pick*
> **To point:** *pick*

and so on until the trace sequence is ended by either pressing *Return* or keying *c* (close) to complete the **TRACE**.

Note: Traces do not appear on screen until after the third point is picked or *Return* pressed. When the third point is selected, the first part of the trace between the first and second picked points appears. In this manner the trace shape does not fully appear until *Return* is pressed or until the trace is closed. Trace lines join at correctly mitred corners irrespective of the angles at which each part meets. The ends of a trace are perpendicular to its edges.

Trace lines become parallel outlines if **TRACE FILL** is **OFF**.

Exercises

1. A two-view orthographic drawing of a pulley is given in Fig. 5.17.

    Copy the given front view and add the sectional view on

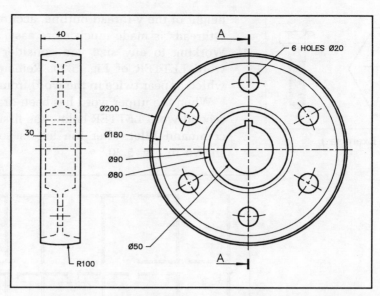

Fig. 5.17 Exercise 1

A–A. Do not include any dimensions, but add a title block which includes details about the drawing.

2. Make an accurate drawing of the detail given in Fig. 5.18. You will need to use commands **array** (p) and **hatch** (u).

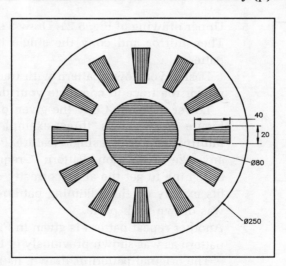

Fig. 5.18 Exercise 2

3. Draw an accurate copy of the EXIT sign given in Fig. 5.19. Choose your own dimensions.

Design and draw another EXIT sign.

Copy the bolt in Fig. 5.19. The v-thread outlines can be accurately drawn by using the command **copy** and selecting the **multiple copies** prompt. If **ortho** is **on** and **snap** is set to the

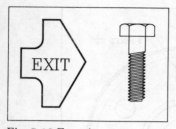

Fig. 5.19 Exercise 3

height of the v-thread outline, accurate drawing of the series of v-threads is made much more easy.

4. Working to any size you consider suitable, copy the upper word LETTER of Fig. 5.20. Remember to copy those letters which appear twice in the word from one drawing of that letter.

   When the upper word has been drawn, use **copy** to produce a second word LETTER below the first. Then, with the aid of the command **fillet**, alter the letters so that serifs are drawn as shown in Fig. 5.20.

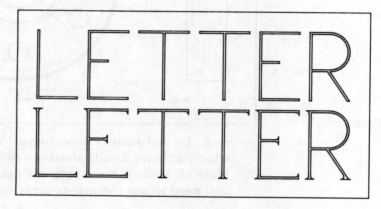

Fig. 5.20 Exercise 4

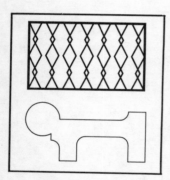

Fig. 5.21 Exercise 5

5. Upper drawing of Fig. 5.21. Draw a single trace line in a zigzag. Then mirror and copy the single trace to produce the given pattern.

   Design your own pattern with trace lines and then copy and mirror the trace to complete your design.

   Lower drawing. Copy the given outline.

6. Figure 5.22 shows three examples of patterns which are multiple copies of a single feature. Pattern 1 can be drawn with any size of polygon. Pattern 2 requires careful planning and designing to get the sizes correctly drawn so that each pattern fits exactly on the adjoining pattern. The original pattern of 3 was drawn with pline.

7. Another repeat pattern is given in Fig. 5.23. This uses the same pattern as was shown previously in Fig. 4.11.

   The original pattern is drawn. Its hatch pattern is AutoCAD's EARTH hatch pattern. This original was then mirrored. The double pattern was then multiple copied to produce the complete pattern. The pattern frame is a trace line.

8. The filled outlines of Fig. 5.24 were drawn with the aid of the commands **solid**, **donut** and **trace**. The semicircular solids are doughnuts which have been halved with the aid of **trim**. First

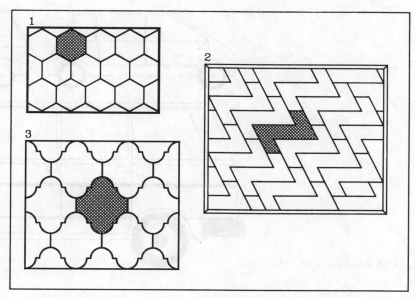

Fig. 5.22 Exercise 6

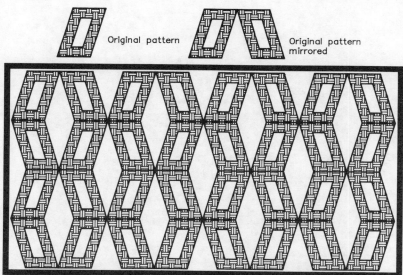

Fig. 5.23 Exercise 7

Fig. 5.24 Exercise 8

draw a line through the centre of a doughnut. Then **trim** it back to the trim line. Finally erase the trim line.

9. Figure 5.25 shows the side views of some vehicles. Design and draw your own car outline. Wheels are **donut**s, sidelines are **trace**s. Hatch patterns could be added to parts of your drawing — e.g. door, windows, etc.

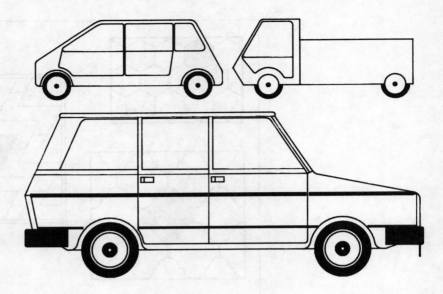

Fig. 5.25 Exercise 9

CHAPTER 6

Wblocks, blocks and inserts

Wblocks

A **wblock** – **w** for written – is written as a drawing file to disc with its own file name, including the drawing file extension *.dwg*. The file is an ordinary drawing file and can be loaded from AutoCAD's **Main menu** under:

2. Edit an EXISTING drawing:

in the same way as any other AutoCAD drawing file if wished.

An example of a WBLOCK

Taking as an example the drawing of the British Standards symbol of a lamp for inclusion in an electrical circuit drawing, Fig. 6.1 shows the sequence for saving a **wblock** drawing file of the symbol to disc.

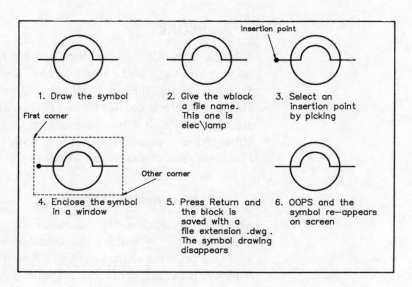

Fig. 6.1 Stages in forming a **BLOCK** or **WBLOCK**

Drawing 1

Draw the symbol in the screen drawing area of the drawing editor. Then call the command **WBLOCK**. The drawing numbers shown below against the responses to the prompts in the command structure refer to the drawing numbers in Fig. 6.1.

> **Command: WBLOCK**
> **File name:** elec\lamp *Keyboard Return (Drawing 2)*
> **Block name:** *Return*
> **Insertion base point:** *pick (Drawing 3)*
> **Select objects:** w *Keyboard Return*
> **First corner:** *pick* **Other corner:** *pick* **4 found.** *(Drawing 4)*
> **Select objects:** *Return (Drawing 5)*
> **Command:**

The drawing of the symbol disappears from the screen and is saved as a drawing file on disc with the file extension *.dwg*. In the example given, the full file name would be

> *c:\acad\elec\lamp.dwg*

Drawing 6

If the symbol drawing is required on screen it can be returned by typing (or selecting) **OOPS** and the symbol reappears. The file on disc – *c:\acad\elec\lamp.dwg* – will, however, not be affected by **OOPS**.

BLOCKs

A **block** is similar to a **wblock**, except that **blocks** are part of the current drawing and, when saved, are included in the current drawing file together with all other drawing details in the current drawing. A **block** cannot be **insert**ed in any drawing other than the drawing in which it has been drawn or saved. **Blocks** therefore are not saved as separate drawing files with their own extensions *.dwg*. The command structure for **block** is the same as for **wblock**.

The command INSERT

Any drawing with a file extension *.dwg* can be **insert**ed into any other drawing by calling the command **insert** and following the resulting prompts at the command line with appropriate responses. A **block**, however, will only respond to the **insert** command if the current drawing contains the **block** to be **insert**ed. When a **wblock**,

block or drawing is being **insert**ed, the drawing appears on screen positioned at the cursor lines intersection at the insertion point saved with the **block**. If a drawing other than a **wblock** or **block** is being inserted, the insertion point will be the coordinate point x, y = (0, 0) of the drawing.

Note that it is only when **dragmode** is **ON** (the default value), that the **block**, **wblock** or drawing appears on screen with its insertion point positioned at the cursor line intersections. If **dragmode** is **ON** then the **wblock**, **block** or drawing can be dragged into position by moving the cursor lines with the pointing device.

The names of all **blocks** which have been drawn with the current drawing can be seen on screen by typing a **?** in response to the first **insert** prompt. In the case of **wblock**s this response to the **?** only applies to those **wblock**s (and other drawings) which have already been inserted into the current drawing.

Example of an INSERT

Taking as an example a **wblock** (or **block**) drawing of a bolt, the sequence of **insert**ing the bolt into a drawing is shown in the six drawings of Fig. 6.2.

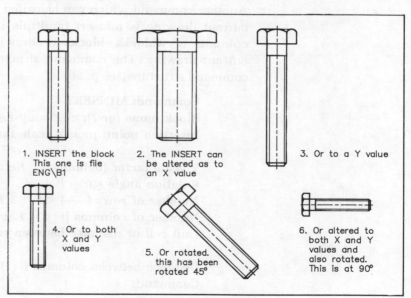

1. INSERT the block This one is file ENG\B1

2. The INSERT can be altered as to an X value

3. Or to a Y value

4. Or to both X and Y values

5. Or rotated. this has been rotated 45°

6. Or altered to both X and Y values and also rotated. This is at 90°

Fig. 6.2 Changing the scale and rotation of an **INSERT**

Drawing 1

Call the command **insert** and key in the filename of the **wblock**. The required **wblock** drawing appears on screen to be dragged into position with the pointer device. The drawing will appear at this stage on screen in faint outlines. The drawing numbers following the responses to the **insert** prompts given below refer to the drawing numbers in Fig. 6.2. Note that the full outlines of the **wblock, block** or drawing do not appear on screen until *Return* is pressed following the **Rotation angle <0>:** prompt at the end of the **insert** command sequence.

> **Command: INSERT**
> **Block name (or ?):** eng\bolt1 *Keyboard Return (Drawing 1)*
> **Insertion point:** *pick* **X scale factor <1>/corner/XYZ:**
> *Return (Drawing 2)*
> **Y scale factor (default=X):** *Return (Drawing 3)*
> **Rotation angle <0>:** *Return (Drawings 5 or 6)*
> **Command:**

The **block, wblock** or drawing appears on screen at the point of insertion and at the scale and rotation angle given in answer to the various responses.

The command MINSERT

Another command which can be called to insert drawings into the current drawing is **minsert** (multiple insert) by which rows and columns of **wblocks, blocks** or drawings can be added to the current drawing. The command structure is similar to the **array** command structure (see p. 66).

> **Command: MINSERT**
> **Block name (or ?):** elec\lamp *Keyboard Return*
> **Insertion point:** *pick* **X scale factor <1>:/corner/XYZ:**
> *Return*
> **Y scale factor (default=X):** *Return*
> **Rotation angle <0>:** *Return*
> **Number of rows (——) <1>:** 3 *Keyboard Return*
> **Number of columns (| | |) <1>:** 4 *Keyboard Return*
> **Unit cell or distance between rows (——):** 40 *Keyboard*
> *Return*
> **Distance between columns (| | |):** 30 *Keyboard Return*
> **Command:**

and the rows and columns of the **block, wblock** or drawing appear on screen. Note that as with **array**, the distances between rows and columns are measured from the central point of the drawing being **insert**ed.

Notes – WBLOCKs, BLOCKs and INSERTs

When this set of commands is in use the following details, rules and restrictions apply:

1. When **wblocks**, **blocks** or drawings are **insert**ed, the drawing appears on screen as a complete entity. The objects which make up the drawing become as if they were a single object. This means that the whole **block** can be **moved**, **copy**ed, **erase**d, **array**ed, etc. as if it were a single object. This can be an advantage if the **insert**ed drawing needs to be acted upon by commands such as **copy**, **move**, etc., but can also be a disadvantage if, for example, the **wblock** or **block** needs to be acted upon by commands such as **stretch**, in which only part of the drawing is to be acted upon.

2. If only part of a **wblock** or **block** is to be altered, it can be changed back to a set of single objects with the command **explode** as follows:

   Command: EXPLODE
   Select block reference, polyline dimension or mesh: *pick*
   Command:

   and the **insert**ed **wblock** or **block** or drawing is converted back into its originally drawn individual set of objects, each of which can then be altered as necessary.
   Note: The **explode** command can also be used on polylines or dimensions (see pp. 23 and 92).

3. **Wblocks**, **blocks** or drawings should be **insert**ed only on to layer 0 (the default layer). If **insert**ed on to any other layer they will take on the colours and linetypes of that layer, which may not be those required.

4. However, if a **wblock**, **block** or drawing is **insert**ed on to a layer other than layer 0, and then **explode**d, the drawing will reappear in its original colours and linetypes.

5. If a layer is **OFF** and part of the drawing being inserted contains details originally constructed on the layer which is **OFF**, then those details will not appear with the drawing when it has been **insert**ed.

6. When a drawing is **insert**ed on to a drawing which does not include layers on which the inserted drawing was constructed, those layers will be automatically made with the insertion.

7. When **insert**ing a drawing made to limits different from those of the current drawing, the inserted drawing may need to be altered in its *x* and *y* scales before it is inserted. Otherwise the

insertion may appear at the wrong scale for the current drawing.

Libraries

The commands **wblock**, **block** and **insert** can be used to speed up the production of drawings if *libraries* of frequently used details are kept as drawing files on disc. This applies particularly to the adding to drawings of details such as: bolts of various sizes to engineering drawings; circuit symbols to electronic and electrical circuit drawings; building symbols to building drawings; pneumatic symbols to pneumatic circuit drawings. Libraries of such drawing details can run to hundreds of drawing files on disc.

Examples of details from libraries and their insertion in drawings are given in the remainder of this chapter. Frequently used symbols may be added to the graphics tablets in an AutoCAD set-up. If this method is adopted the symbols can be inserted into drawings by merely pointing at the symbol on the tablet with the pointing device.

Note: AutoCAD software files are normally held on a hard disc (usually named c:), in a directory normally named *acad*. Libraries could be held on your work disc (see p. 27) in directories:

Engineering drawing details	*a:\eng*
Electrical drawing symbols	*a:\elec*
Building drawing symbols	*a:\build*
Pneumatic circuit symbols	*a:\pneu*

and so on according to the purpose for which the drawing files are being held in the library.

Examples from libraries

Engineering drawings

Figure 6.3 shows a few of the bolts, studs, countersunk and cheese-headed screws from a library of engineering parts, drawn to conform with the British Standard BS:308. The drawings of Fig. 6.3 include the positions of the drawing insertion points and file names. The insertion points were automatically filed with the **wblock** or **block** when it was saved.

Figure 6.4 is an assembly drawing of a pipe sleeve in which the bolts, nuts and washers have been **insert**ed from a library of **wblock**s. First, the outlines of the two parts of the assembly were

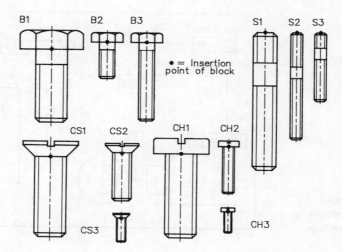

● = Insertion
point of block

Fig. 6.3 Example of part of a
WBLOCK library

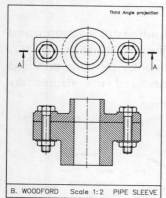

Fig. 6.4 An example of the
use of **INSERT** in an
engineering drawing

Fig. 6.5 Example of part of
an engineering drawing
geometrical symbols library

drawn, then the bolts, nuts and washers were **insert**ed at correct
positions within the outlines.

Figure 6.5 shows part of a library of **wblock**s for including details
of geometrical tolerances in engineering drawings. Each **wblock** is
given a name and its insertion point is shown.

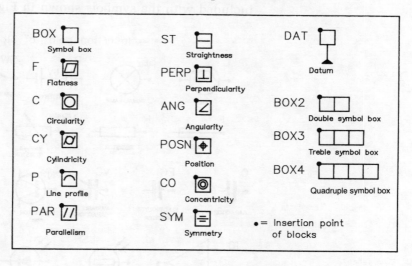

Figure 6.6 shows details from three drawings which have had
geometrical tolerances added from the library, part of which was
given in Fig. 6.5. Figures, letters and leader lines were added after
wblocks parts from the library had been **insert**ed.

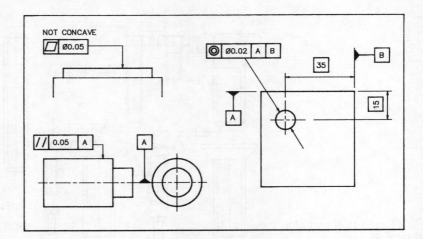

Fig. 6.6 Examples of geometrical tolerances **insert**ed into drawings

Electrical/electronic circuits

The British Standard BS:3939 includes hundreds of electronic and electrical installation symbols. A few of these are given in Fig. 6.7, which is part of a library of BS:3939 symbols. As with previous illustrations of libraries, insertion points and file names are included with the symbols shown in Fig. 6.7.

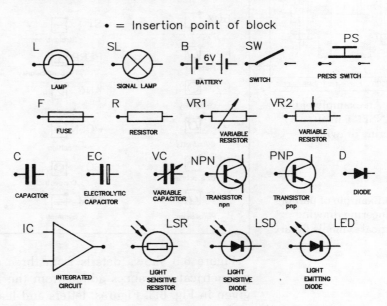

Fig. 6.7 Example of part of a library of electrical and electronic symbols

Figure 6.8 is a drawing of two simple electronic circuits constructed from **wblock**s held in the BS:3939 library, shown in part in Fig. 6.7.

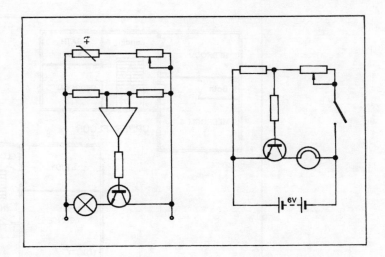

Fig. 6.8 Two simple
electronic circuits drawn by
INSERTing from a library

Building drawings

Figure 6.9 is part of a set of drawing files in a library of British
Standards building drawing symbols. Figure 6.10 is a building plan
of a two-storey house constructed from the drawings held in this
library. Walls and partitions in these plans were added after the
symbols had been inserted in the drawing. The thicknesses of these
two items were determined with the aid of the **offset** command.

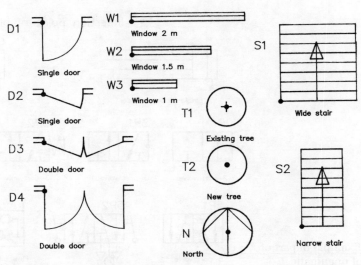

Fig. 6.9 Example of part of a
building drawing symbols
library

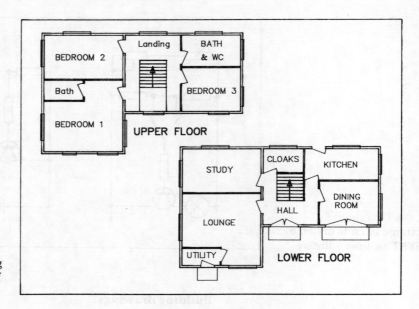

Fig. 6.10 A building drawing
constructed from a library of
symbols

Pneumatic circuits

Part of a library of files of some British Standards symbols
representing components for inclusion in pneumatic circuit drawings is given in Fig. 6.11. File names and insertion points are
included with the drawings.

Figures 6.12 and 6.13 are two circuit drawings – one of a
pneumatics circuit for the control of drilling depth, the second of a

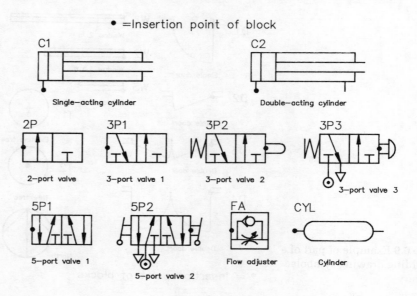

Fig. 6.11 Example of part of
a library of pneumatic
component symbols

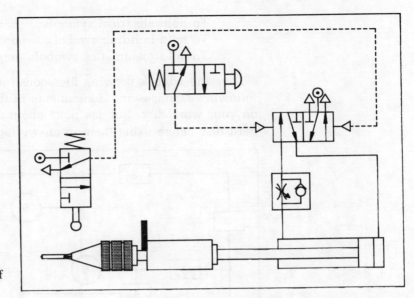

Fig. 6.12 An example of a simple pneumatics circuit constructed from a library of symbols

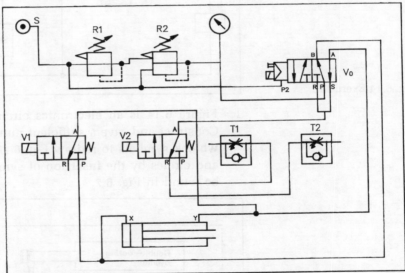

Fig. 6.13 An example of a hydraulics circuit constructed from a library of symbols

hydraulics circuit. The hydraulics circuit of Fig. 6.13 was partly constructed from the files held in the pneumatics symbols library. Details not included in the library were added later.

Exercises

With the MS.DOS command **md** (or **mkdir**) make new directories on your work disc:

To hold engineering symbols *a:\eng*

To hold electrical symbols   *a:\elec*
To hold building symbols   *a:\build*
To hold pneumatics symbols *a:\pneu*

Save the **wblock** drawing files constructed when answering the following exercises and assignments in the appropriate directories on your work disc. But see p. 27 about copying these files to the hard disc before using them in answering exercises.

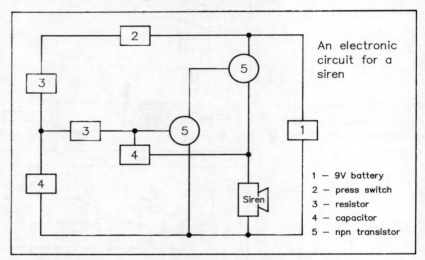

Fig. 6.14 Exercise 1

1. Figure 6.14 is an electronics circuit drawn without symbols. Construct and save a sufficient number of electrical/electronics **wblock** symbols to redraw Fig. 6.15 by replacing the rectangle and circles by the **insert**ion of symbols. Suitable symbols will be found in Fig. 6.7.

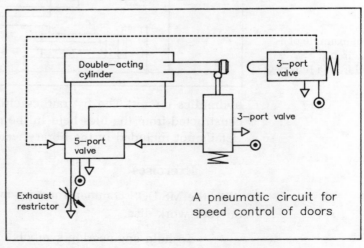

Fig. 6.15 Exercise 2

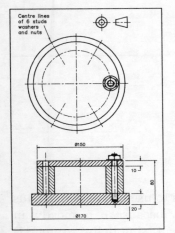

Fig. 6.16 Exercise 3

2. Figure 6.15 is an incomplete pneumatics circuit in which details of the valves and cylinder are missing. Copy Fig. 6.15. Construct and save a sufficient number of **wblock** drawings to **insert** in the drawing to complete the circuit. Symbols can be copied from Fig. 6.11.

3. Figure 6.16 is an incomplete front view and plan of an assembly.
   (a) Copy Fig. 6.16;
   (b) Complete the drawing by adding the six studs, nuts and washers to the plan and the studs, nuts and washers to the front view.

   Note: With AutoCAD, the additions could be made by using commands such as **array**, **copy**, **move**. In this exercise, construct separate drawings of the front views and plans of the stud, nut and washer and save them as **wblocks**. Then **insert** these saved drawings into their positions in the drawing.

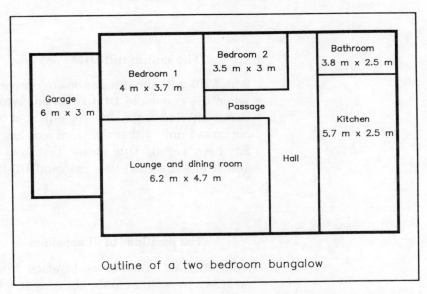

Fig. 6.17 Exercise 4

4. An outline drawing of a two-bedroom bungalow is given in Fig. 6.17. It was drawn with the aid of CAD software using the **pline** and **text** commands.
   (a) Construct and save a sufficient number of **wblock** drawings of building symbols (see Fig. 6.9);
   (b) Make an accurate building plan of the bungalow with **insert**ed building symbols for doors, windows, etc. placed in well-designed positions.

CHAPTER 7

Dimensioning

Introduction

One of the easiest of AutoCAD's facilities to use is that which adds dimensions to drawings. This is mainly because it is mostly an automatic process. Despite this apparent simplicity, AutoCAD dimensioning involves a large number of variables, many of which can be set by the operator.

The command DIM

AutoCAD will add dimensions to drawings in an automatic fashion when the command **DIM** is called. When this command is at the command line of the drawing editor, it will continue as the current command until either the word *exit* has been keyed, or until *Ctrl/C* has been keyed. This means that after each dimension has been added to a drawing, the command **DIM:** automatically reappears.

The positions of dimensions

AutoCAD can be requested to place dimensions in many different positions in relation to the drawing to which they are being added. Figure 7.1 gives the names of the **DIM** prompts to obtain the variety of positions common to technical drawings. Each prompt can be called with an abbreviation – the first three letters of the positional name. Figure 7.1 also shows the actual form of dimensioning resulting from these positional prompts. The actual positions of the dimension figures will depend upon the way in which the **DIM** variables have been set. Figure 7.1 includes the **DIM** settings for the dimensions shown.

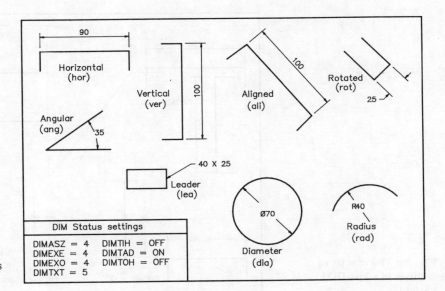

Fig. 7.1 Some of the options available with **DIM**

DIM variables

When configuring a sheet size for AutoCAD, common practice is to include the dimensioning variables which are those most often employed at the workstation. When AutoCAD is loaded into the computer at a workstation by keying *acad* (usually), the software has normally been configured so that the sheet size of drawing commonly worked at the station appears on screen in the drawing editor. There are some thirty to forty dimensioning variables with this software. In this book, we will deal only with those which are most frequently employed to produce the type of dimensioning of drawings most often used at student level. The way in which some of these variables affect the positions of dimension figures is shown in Figs 7.2 and 7.3.

The settings of all the **DIM** variables can be seen by calling the command **DIM** and then keying or picking the prompt **status**. The drawing editor clears and a list appears on screen with the **DIM** variable settings. All the variables begin with the letters **DIM**. When set, these control features of dimensioning such as arrow size, whether dimensions are to appear above or in the middle of dimension lines, the size of the extension beyond dimension lines, the gap between drawing and dimension extension lines, etc. Figures 7.1–7.3 show the settings of those **DIM** variables most likely to be needed.

To set a **DIM** variable, call the command **DIM** and then key the **DIM** variable name. Thus to change the variable **DIMASZ** (arrow size):

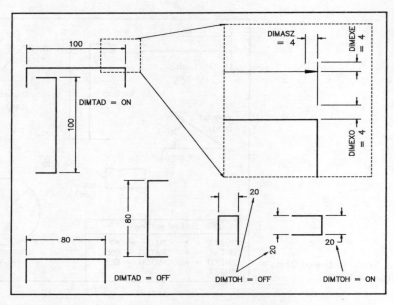

Fig. 7.2 The results of settings of some **DIM** variables

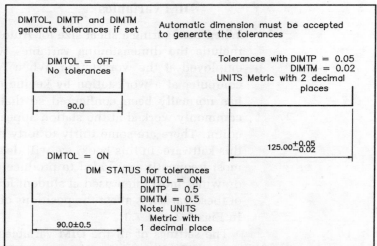

Fig. 7.3 The results of settings of some other **DIM** variables

Command: DIM *Return*
Dim: dimasz *Keyboard Return*
Current value <4.0000> New value: 6 *Keyboard Return*
Dim:

and the variable is set until again changed.

The DIM command sequence

Figure 7.4 shows the sequence of prompts and responses to obtain a dimension on a drawing when **DIM** is called. This sequence is common to all the most frequently used dimensioning methods.

Note: As each response is given to the prompts, either by a point being picked or stated in x, y coordinate numbers, or when *Return* is pressed, the screen response is automatic. Only when the prompt

Dimension text <90.0000>:

appears, can a keyed response be given. The figure (or letters) keyed here will be displayed in their correct position with the complete dimension on screen. The figures/letters need not be the same as those given in the prompt brackets. Details such as:

M10 × 1.5; TOLERANCE to 0.002; DATUM; 100 mm;

can be keyed in at this prompt, followed by *Return*. If *Return* is pressed without keying in your own figures or letters, the bracketed figures will appear as the required dimension.

When the sequence has been completed and the dimension has appeared in its position on screen, the **Dim:** prompt reappears at the command line, ready for the next dimension to be drawn on screen.

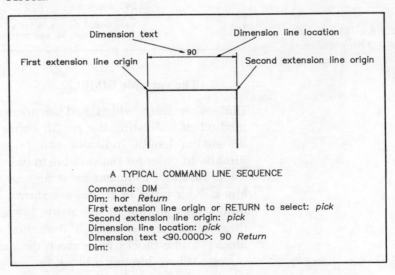

Fig. 7.4 The **DIM** command
line sequence

Figure 7.5 is a drawing which has been dimensioned with the aid of AutoCAD. Note that some modifications were made after the dimensioning had been completed. This was thought necessary in this example because:

(a) the operator preferred his own diameter symbols to those automatically produced by AutoCAD;

(b) the operator wished to alter the positions of some figures from the positions automatically allocated by AutoCAD.

In the example given (Fig. 7.5) horizontal, vertical, diameter, radius and leader dimensions were included with the drawing.

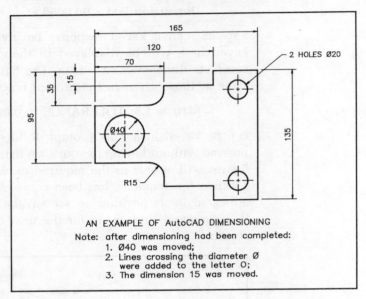

AN EXAMPLE OF AutoCAD DIMENSIONING

Note: after dimensioning had been completed:
1. Ø40 was moved;
2. Lines crossing the diameter Ø were added to the letter O;
3. The dimension 15 was moved.

Fig. 7.5 An example of AutoCAD dimensioning

The variable DIMBLK

Dimension lines which end in arrows are not always the best method of indicating the length being dimensioned. The type of dimension length indicator can be changed with the variable **dimblk**. In order for the variable to be effective, the required type of dimension end indicator must first be drawn and then saved as a **block**. Four types of arrows are shown in Fig. 7.6, which includes dimensions ending in the arrow loaded when **dim** is called and three other 'arrows' which were first drawn and then saved as **block**s. These blocks were given the names 1, 2 and 3.

Note: When drawing a **block** for saving as a dimension arrow, it must be constructed with each part drawn to one unit length. Then when the block is loaded for dimensioning purposes, the unit lengths will assume the sizes given by the variable **dimasz** (arrow length).

If an arrow block has not previously been saved, the variable **dimblk** can only return the normal arrow type. Common practice is for several dimension arrow types to be loaded with the sheet size which appears when AutoCAD is loaded into the computer. If this is not so, then draw the required arrow to single unit sizes and save it as a **block** with a name of a figure – 1, 2, etc.

To load a different dimension arrow follow the sequence:

> **Command: DIM** *Return*
> **Dim:** dimblk *Return*
> **Current value** <> **New value:** 1 *block name keyed in*
> *Return*
>
> **Dim:**

If the value is say, 1 or 2, etc. and the original type of arrow is wanted, key a full stop (.) as a response to **New value:**.

In Fig. 7.6 four types of dimension arrows have been used for the dimensions.

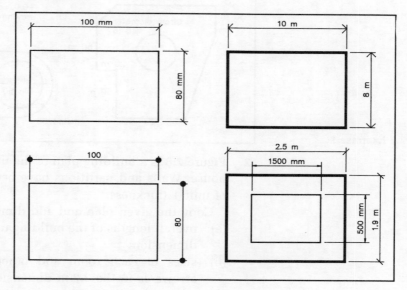

Fig. 7.6 Different types of dimensioning 'arrows'

Other DIM details

1. If a mistake is made when dimensioning a drawing, and it is spotted immediately after it has been made, keying a u (undo) erases all of the last dimension drawn.
2. Set **style** (text) and the layer on which dimensions are to be drawn before entering the **DIM** command sequence.
3. If instead of calling the **DIM** command, the command **DIM1** is called, as each dimension appears on screen the command line returns to **Command:** and not to **Dim:**. **DIM1** is of value when the operator wishes to add just one or only a few dimension(s) to a drawing.

Exercises

1. Copy the four outlines of Fig. 7.7 and, in place of the size indications, include accurate dimensions with the aid of the AutoCAD **DIM** command.

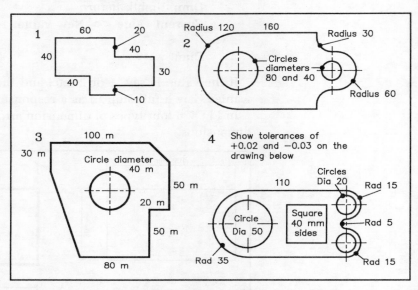

Fig. 7.7 Exercise 1

2. Figure 7.8 is a building plan of the upper storey of a two-storey house. Walls and partitions have been drawn with pline lines of unit 1 thickness.

   Copy the given plan and add dimensions as follows:
   (a) overall lengths of the building using arrows as in the 9.3 m dimension;
   (b) sizes of each room and other spaces with dimension arrows as in the 3.2 m dimension.

3. If you have drawn an answer to Exercise 5 of Chapter 4, reload the drawing as an *existing* drawing and fully dimension the views.

Setting up drawing sheet files

AutoCAD can be configured so that a file *acad.dwg* automatically loads when commencing a new drawing under

Main menu
1. Begin a NEW drawing

when AutoCAD is loaded. The configuration is carried out under

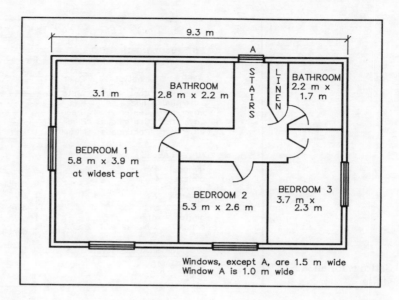

Fig. 7.8 Exercise 2

Main menu

8. Configure AutoCAD

Normal practice is to design the drawing represented by *acad.dwg* to appear in the drawing editor as suitable for drawing on a sheet size such as A4 or A3. The specific sheet size, the drawings and the variables associated with *acad.dwg* will depend upon the type of drawing usually produced at the workstation.

Another method of ensuring that the drawing editor is set to the type of drawing sheet size wished to be used is to make up several sheet files – say one for A4, another for A3, yet another for A2. These files could be *a:\sheet_a4.dwg*, *a:\sheet_a3.dwg*, or whatever other name is thought suitable. Each of these can have its own title block, headings, set variables, or any other feature which one wishes always to see on one's drawings.

Figure 7.9 shows the settings suitable for either an *acad.dwg* file for automatic loading when AutoCAD is called, or for **SAVE**ing as *a:\sheet a3   dwg* file. The *a:* shows that the file will be **SAVE**d to your work disc.

To make up such a sheet file, key in either *acad* or *a:\sheet_a3* in response to:

> **Enter selection:_** 1 *Keyboard Return*
> **Enter name of drawing_** a:\sheet_a3 *Keyboard Return*

under the **Main menu**.

Then proceed as follows:

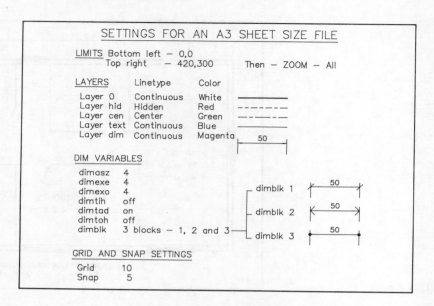

Fig. 7.9 Settings for an A3 size sheet file

1. Call the command **LIMITS** and set the **Lower left corner:** to x, y 0, 0 and the **Upper right corner:** to x, y = 420, 300. Why these limits? Because an A3 sheet is 420 by 297 mm. If the x, y coordinates are set 420, 300, each x and y figure on the A3 sheet will represent 1mm in the screen drawing area of the drawing editor;

2. Call the command **ZOOM:** and zoom **All**. This sets the screen drawing editor to the limits 420, 300;

3. Call the command **LAYER:** and Make a new layer *hid* with a linetype *hidden* and of colour *red*. Make several layers as shown in Fig. 7.9;

4. Set the **dim** variables as shown in Fig. 7.9 by calling the command **DIM:** and then each **dim** variable in turn;

5. Set **GRID:** to 10 and **SNAP:** to 5 or any other settings thought suitable;

6. Finally **SAVE** the drawing. This can be done by answering either *acad* or *a:\sheet_a3* at the command line when **SAVE:** is called or by just pressing the *Return* key at **SAVE:** – the file will then have the name given in response to **Enter name of drawing:** given before the drawing commenced.

Note: If you are working at a school or college workstation or at one used by other people, do *not* make up your own *acad.dwg* file. If you do so, every time anyone else uses the workstation to commence a new drawing they will probably get your *acad.dwg* file as a start-up drawing screen. This may cause difficulties for other people. If you make up your own sheet size files save them to your work disc in Drive a:.

A sheet file which you may wish to consider is one that includes a border margin, a title block and various details which you may wish always to appear when using AutoCAD. Such a drawing is shown in Fig. 7.10.

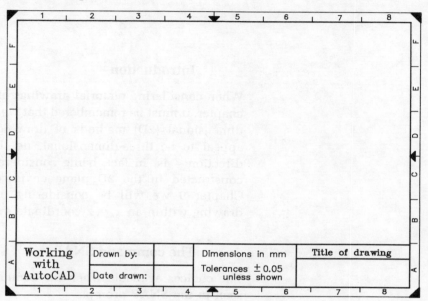

Working with AutoCAD	Drawn by:		Dimensions in mm	Title of drawing
	Date drawn:		Tolerances ± 0.05 unless shown	

Fig. 7.10 An example of a drawing sheet saved as a sheet file

If such a drawing were drawn and its file saved as *acad.dwg*, it would appear when AutoCAD was started up and a *new* drawing was requested under the **Main menu**.

CHAPTER 8

Pictorial drawing

Introduction

When considering pictorial drawings of the type dealt with in this
chapter, it must be remembered that we are really dealing with two-
dimensional (2D) methods of drawing. Even though the results
appear to be three-dimensional, no third dimension – in the z
direction – is, in fact, being considered. The drawings are being
constructed in the 2D plane envisaged by x, y coordinates. In
Chapter 9 we will be considering true three-dimensional (3D)
drawing within an x, y, z coordinate system.

The command SNAP

The choices available when the command **SNAP** is called can be
seen in the **SNAP** prompts

Command: SNAP
Snap spacing or ON/OFF/Aspect/Rotate/Style <0.0000>:

The responses keyed in answer to these prompts have the
following effects:

ON/OFF – decides whether **snap** is **ON** or **OFF**.
Aspect – keying an a allows both horizontal and vertical spacings
    of the **snap** points to be set independently of each other. The
    snap points will assume a rectangular form determined by the
    figures given in answer to further prompts which appear when a
    is keyed;
Rotate – keying an r allows the whole **snap** system to be rotated
    around a base point. When r is keyed followed by *Return*, first a
    Base point: is requested – this will usually be $x, y = 0, 0$. Then a
    Rotation angle: can be keyed in – an angle in degrees. Then in
    response to *Return* being pressed, the whole **snap** system then
    rotates around the base point at the rotation angle, while

retaining its rectangular or square settings.

Style – if an *s* is keyed a further prompt appears requesting whether the **Standard** or the **Isometric** style of **snap** points is required. Keying an *s* results in a request to set the **snap** spacings – this time they will be set in a square system, parallel to the screen edges. Keying an *i* results in the **snap** settings being set isometrically – at angles of 30° to horizontal to both left and right. The distances between the **snap** points can be set by stating the vertical spacing in response to the prompt **Vertical spacing:** which appears at the command line when *i Return* has been keyed.

Note: If **GRID** is **on**, and either **snap rotate** or **snap isometric** is called, **grid** points appear and take up the positions determined by the **rotate** or **isometric** angles. **GRID** and **SNAP** may be set to different spacings, but assume the same angles.

When drawing in an isometric **snap** system two further commands will be needed to obtain an accurate isometric drawing. The first of these is **ISOPLANE**, to determine whether one is working on the left, on the top or on the right-hand sides of an isometric drawing. The command follows the pattern

> **Command: ISOPLANE** *Return*
> **Left/Top/Right/<Toggle>:** t *Keyboard Return*
> **Command:**

Either key in *t*, *l* or *r* or press *Return* to decide which face is to be constructed, or to toggle between the sides or top in the order left, top, right. Note that the cursor lines show which side has been selected by assuming the correct stance for the side.

Note: The **isoplane** can also be toggled between *t*, *l* and *r* by pressing keys *Ctrl+E*.

The second command which is suitable for isometric drawing is **ELLIPSE** (see p. 21). When drawing in isometric, circles assume the shape of isometric ellipses.

Note: Isometric circles can only be drawn when in the isometric **snap** mode. When in this **snap** mode the command **ELLIPSE** brings the following to the command line:

> **Command: ELLIPSE**
> **<Axis endpoint 1>/Center/Isocircle:**

Keying an *i* in response allows the isometric circle (ellipse) appropriate to the **isoplane** in action, to be drawn on screen. Figure 8.1 shows ellipses as they would appear in their respective isoplanes.

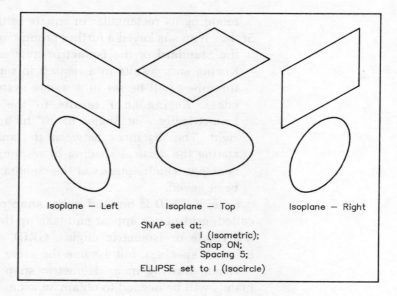

Isoplane — Left   Isoplane — Top   Isoplane — Right

SNAP set at:
    I (Isometric);
    Snap ON;
    Spacing 5;
ELLIPSE set to I (Isocircle)

Fig. 8.1 Examples of
ISOPLANE settings

Isometric drawing

Isometric drawing with AutoCAD follows the same procedures as
when drawing by hand with instruments. No special skill is
required. After setting **SNAP** to isometric and selecting the correct
isoplanes in turn as the drawing develops, pictorial drawings such
as the simple examples given in Fig. 8.2 can be readily drawn.
Isometric drawing is made easier if both **SNAP** and **GRID** are **ON**,
because they then give an accurate guide to the correct positioning
of features such as the ends of lines and the centres and axes of
isocircles.

Because this is a 2D method of drawing, command systems
described in previous chapters can all be employed when
constructing pictorial drawings — e.g. **erase**, **trim**, **break**, **copy**,
move, etc. Another system which is also available for pictorial
drawing is the relative coordinate system, in which the sizes of
parts of a drawing are determined by the relative coordinate figures
seen on the status line when coords is ON.

Exploded isometric drawings such as that given in Fig. 8.3 are
also possible. Any form of exploded drawing is made easier when
using AutoCAD because of the simplicity with which good
positioning of the parts in relation to each other can be achieved by
taking advantage of the **MOVE** and **COPY** commands systems.

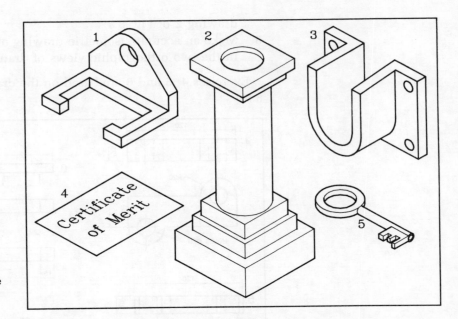

Fig. 8.2 Examples of simple
AutoCAD isometric
drawings

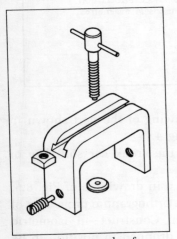

Fig. 8.3 An example of a
more detailed isometric
drawing

Fig. 8.4 Exercises 1–3

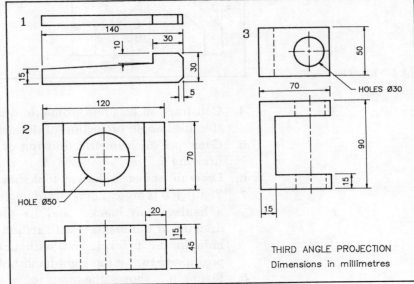

THIRD ANGLE PROJECTION
Dimensions in millimetres

Exercises

Exercises 1, 2 and 3 are based on the drawings in Fig. 8.4.

1. Construct an accurate isometric drawing of the gib key shown by a two-view orthographic projection.
2. Construct an accurate isometric drawing of the slide shown in

drawing 2 of Fig. 8.4.

3. Make an accurate isometric drawing of the angle bracket given in the two orthographic views of drawing 3.

Exercises 4, 5 and 6 are based on the drawings 4, 5 and 6 of Fig. 8.5.

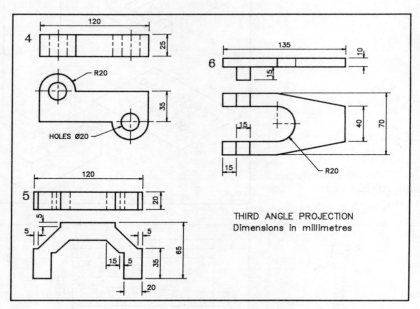

Fig. 8.5 Exercises 4–6

4. Construct an accurate isometric drawing of the part shown in the third angle projection of drawing 4.
5. Construct an isometric drawing of the crank car shift key of drawing 5.
6. Draw in isometric the key tool shown in drawing 6 of Fig. 8.5.
7. Figure 8.6 is an exploded third angle orthographic projection of a haulage pin bracket and its pin. Construct an isometric drawing of the bracket, with its pin dropped in position in its hole in the bracket, and with one of the attachment bolts positioned in the top right-hand hole of the bracket.
8. Figure 8.7 shows the parts of a lightweight jacking device drawn in an exploded orthographic projection. The slide (part 4) is first dropped into the square hole in the body (part 1). The pin (part 3) is placed in the pin holder (part 2) and the pin holder is then inserted into the square hole above the slide (part 4) already in the hole. The screw (part 5) is screwed into its threaded hole in the body and when tightened the sloping face of the slide acts on the sloping face of the pin holder to

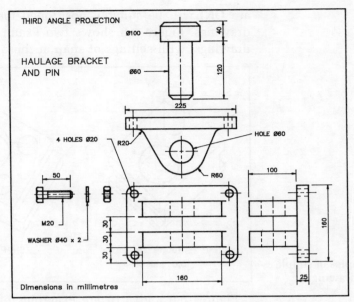

Fig. 8.6 Exercise 7

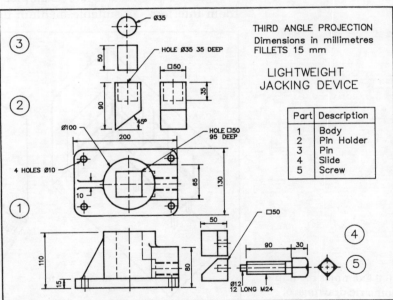

Fig. 8.7 Exercise 8

push it and its pin upwards.

Draw an isometric drawing of the assembled jacking device.

Planometric drawing

If the command **SNAP** is called and the **snap** points rotated through either 45° or through 30°, the **snap** points (and **grid** points if they are **ON**) will be suitably positioned for constructing planometric drawings. Figure 8.8 shows two examples of simple planometric drawings, with settings of **snap** at these two angles.

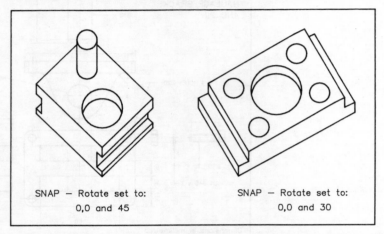

SNAP – Rotate set to:
0,0 and 45

SNAP – Rotate set to:
0,0 and 30

Fig. 8.8 Examples of simple planometric drawings

Figures 8.9 and 8.10 are examples of planometric drawings or room interiors – a suitable medium for this form of drawing.

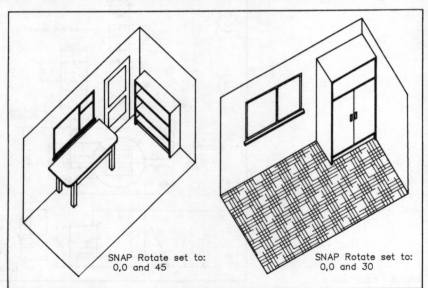

SNAP Rotate set to:
0,0 and 45

SNAP Rotate set to:
0,0 and 30

Fig. 8.9 Examples of simple planometric drawings of room interiors

Exercises

1. Figure 8.11 is a plan of a fitted kitchen drawn on a 0.5 m grid. With the grid as a guide to sizes, construct planometric drawings as seen from above and viewed first in the direction of arrow 1, then in the direction of arrow 2.

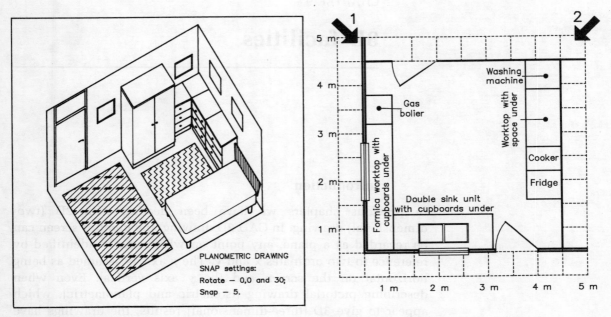

PLANOMETRIC DRAWING
SNAP settings:
Rotate – 0,0 and 30;
Snap – 5.

Fig. 8.10 A more detailed
planometric drawing

Fig. 8.11 Exercise 9

2. Take measurements and notes of the sizes and furniture in your own bedroom and then make a planometric drawing from these measurements and notes.

3D facilities

Introduction

In previous chapters we have been dealing with 2D (two-dimensional) drawing. In CAD 2D drawing, the monitor screen can be regarded as a plane, any point on which can be identified by reference to two ordinates x and y. The x axis is assumed as being horizontal on the screen and the y axis vertical. Even when describing pictorial drawing (isometric and planometric), which appear to give 3D (three-dimensional) results, the drawings have been constructed in a 2D plane, with points identified by x, y coordinates.

With AutoCAD, true 3D drawing is possible. In 3D, each point of a drawing is uniquely determined by three coordinate points x, y and z. The x and y axes are assumed to be horizontal and vertical on the monitor screen and the z axis is assumed to be as if perpendicular to the screen. AutoCAD 3D drawings appear on screen as *wire frames*, in which x, y, z coordinate points are jointed together by lines.

3D drawing

Five basic command systems are available for constructing and viewing AutoCAD 3D wire frames. These are **ELEVATION**, **3DFACE**, **3DLINE**, **VPOINT** and **HIDE**. Of these five, the first three are for 3D construction. When a wire frame has been constructed, it can be viewed from different directions with the aid of **VPOINT**. With some 3D drawings, unwanted lines behind faces can be removed with the **HIDE** command.

The command 3DFACE

3DFACE is for constructing surfaces. Lines behind 3Dfaces can be hidden with the command **hide**. All 3dfaces are built up in either triangles or quadrilaterals. A 3Dface can be constructed by keying in x, y, z coordinates of its corners or by picking its corners on **ELEVATION** surfaces.

The command 3DLINE

3DLINE allows 3D drawings consisting of straight lines to be constructed. Lines behind faces produced with the aid of **3DLINE** will not be hidden when **HIDE** is called. The end points of each **3DLINE** must be described in terms of x, y, z coordinates.

The command VPOINT

With **VPOINT** any 3D drawing can be viewed from a variety of positions. Note that if a 2D drawing is viewed with the aid of this command, only its outlines on the x, y plane will be seen. When **VPOINT** is called, the viewing direction can be given in terms of x, y, z coordinates. If keying in the figures for the coordinates, each figure is that which is a position on the x, y, z axes from which the coordinate point 0, 0, 0 (the origin) is seen. Thus a figure of $-1, -1, 1$ is looking at the coordinate point 0, 0, 0 from the left ($-$ve) along the x axis, from the front ($-$ve) looking along the y axis and from above ($+$ve) looking along the z axis. A figure of 1, 1, 1 is looking from the right ($+$ve) along the x axis, looking from behind ($+$ve) along the y axis and looking from above ($+$ve) along the z axis. When wishing to view a 3D drawing from below the figure for z must be negative. Thus **VPOINT** $-1, -1, -1$ gives a viewing point from left, from in front and from below.

When a 3D drawing is viewed with **VPOINT**, lines behind 3dfaces can be erased (hidden) by calling the command **HIDE**.

Examples of 3DFACE, 3DLINE, VPOINT and HIDE

Figure 9.1 shows:

1. The drawing editor when **3DFACE** is called;
2. A 3D drawing as it appears when it has been constructed with the aid of the command **3DFACE**;
3. The same drawing after **VPOINT** has been called and $-1, -1, 1$ keyed and after **HIDE** has been called.

Figure 9.2 is similar to Fig. 9.1, but it has been constructed with **3DLINE**s. Taking up the same viewing point with **VPOINT**, it can

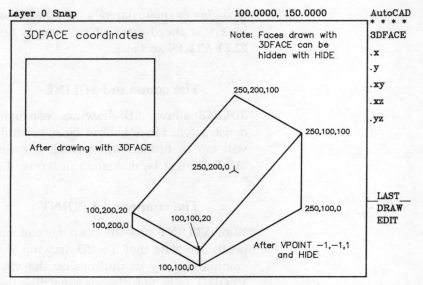

Fig. 9.1 A 3D drawing
constructed with **3DFACE**

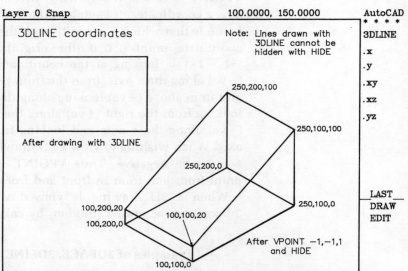

Fig. 9.2 A 3D drawing
constructed with **3DLINE**

be seen that lines behind the faces of the drawing cannot be hidden
with the command **HIDE**.

When drawing with the aid of **3DFACE** or **3DLINE**, any points
picked with a pointing device will be assumed as being on the x, y
plane and so having a z coordinate value of 0. Any 3D point which
does not have a z coordinate of 0 must either:

1. Have all three coordinate points x, y and z keyed in response to
    prompts with the commands; or

2. The point can be chosen by picking a point in the on-screen drawing area after first selecting one of the coordinate choices from the on-screen menu area.

The on-screen menus associated with these two commands are shown in both Figs 9.1 and 9.2. To draw the upper left vertical line of Figs 9.1 or 9.2:

1. Call **3DLINE** (or **3DFACE**);
2. *Pick* the point 100, 200 to fix one end of the line (or face) at 100, 200, 0;
3. Select **.xy** from the on-screen menu;
4. *Pick* the same point on screen. This will determine the x, y position of the 3D point;
5. When **.xy of (need Z):** appears at the command line, key in the z coordinate 20.

The 3D line has now been drawn (or the edge of a 3dface) between the coordinate points 100, 100, 0 and 100, 200, 20.

The command ELEVATION

When the command **ELEVATION** is called, the following appears at the command line:

> **Command: ELEV**
> **New current elevation <0.0000):** *Return*
> **New current thickness <0.0000):** 50 *Return*
> **Command:**

Any object drawn will then assume a height of 50 units extruded above the original x, y plane. The extrusions can be made to appear as 3D wire frames viewed in any direction with the facilities offered by the command **VPOINT**.

ELEV extrusions can only have thickness (height) perpendicular to the x, y plane. They cannot be called to produce thickness in x or y directions.

ELEV extrusions are made up of **3DFACE**s. Lines behind them can be hidden by calling the command **HIDE**. Note, however, that only those hidden details that are *behind* the *vertical* **ELEV**ations can be removed by **HIDE**.

ELEVation extrusions can have a thickness with a new elevation either starting above or below the original x, y plane. Thus the following:

Command: ELEV
New current elevation <0.0000): 20 *Return*
New current thickness <0.0000): 50 *Return*
Command:

sets the drawing editor so that objects drawn will have a thickness of 50 units, with their bases at 20 units above the original x, y plane. Note that the top of the **ELEV**ation extrusion will be 70 units above the x, y plane.

Note: The command system **ELEVATION** is not available from AutoCAD release 11 onwards. Results similar to those achieved with **ELEVATION** can be obtained with the command system **TABSURF** (p. 146). With the aid of the **TABSURF** command system used in conjunction with the **UCS** (Ch. 10), extrusions can be constructed in any direction within the x, y, z 3D coordinate environment.

Examples of ELEVATION 3D drawings

In the drawings of Fig. 9.3, **ELEV** was set to 0 and 30, or 0 and 50, or 0 and 60. Various **DRAW** commands were then selected to obtain the shapes shown. This resulted in the plan views of the objects given in Fig. 9.3. Note that each of these plans has a height in the z direction formed by the appropriate **ELEV new elevation** and **thickness** figures.

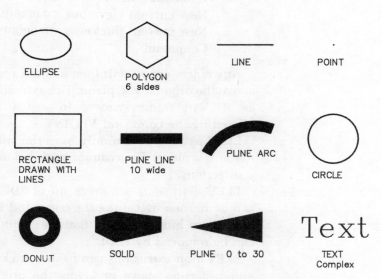

Fig. 9.3 Objects and shapes drawn with various AutoCAD commands on **ELEV**ations

The command **VPOINT** was called and −1, −1, 1 keyed as a response. This response produced a 3D view as seen from the left, front and above. The command **HIDE** was then called and this removed all possible hidden lines. The resulting view is shown in Fig. 9.4.

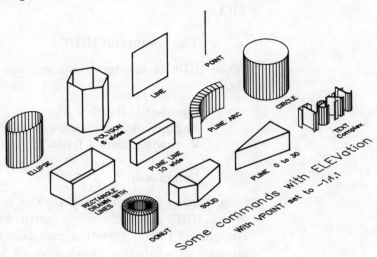

Fig. 9.4 The objects and shapes of Fig. 9.3 viewed from a **VPOINT** viewing position

Figure 9.4 shows that the extruded elevations of various types of objects produce 3D views as follows:

ELLIPSE – made up of a number of 3dfaces. The rear part of the 3D ellipse can be seen;

POLYGON – made up of a number of 3dfaces, with the rear of the 3D view also showing as 3Dfaces;

LINE – forms a single 3Dface;

POINT – extrudes to a single vertical line;

RECTANGLE – made up of four LINEs – forms a box of four 3dfaces;

PLINE – formed from several 3dfaces. Hidden lines are all hidden with **HIDE**;

PLINE ARC – made up of a number of pline segments, each of which is made up from 3dfaces;

CIRCLE – appears as if its top is a 3dface;

DONUT – a number of segments each of which is a composite series of 3dfaces;

SOLID – note that its surfaces are no longer **FILL**ed (compare with Fig. 9.3) and now show as 3dfaces;

PLINE – an example of a pline starting at 0 and ending with 30 units of width;

TEXT – text also assumes shapes made up from a number of 3dfaces.

Note: **PLINE**s and **SOLID**s do not show as **FILL**ed surfaces when in **VPOINT** viewing positions. Neither can **VPOINT** views be **FILL**ed.

The command HIDE

When **HIDE** is selected, the command line of the drawing editor shows

Command: HIDE
Regenerating drawing.
Removing hidden lines: 75 *(multiples of 25s appearing automatically)*
Command:

No further action is needed. The hiding occurs automatically. When **HIDE** is called for a particularly complex 3D drawing, completion of the operation may take a considerable time. If any changes are made in a drawing which has had features hidden, the hidden lines reappear when *Return* is pressed to complete the change.

Further examples of 3D drawings

Figures 9.5 and 9.6 contain examples of simple 3D drawings made with the commands **ELEV**, **3DLINE** and **3DFACE**. They are shown

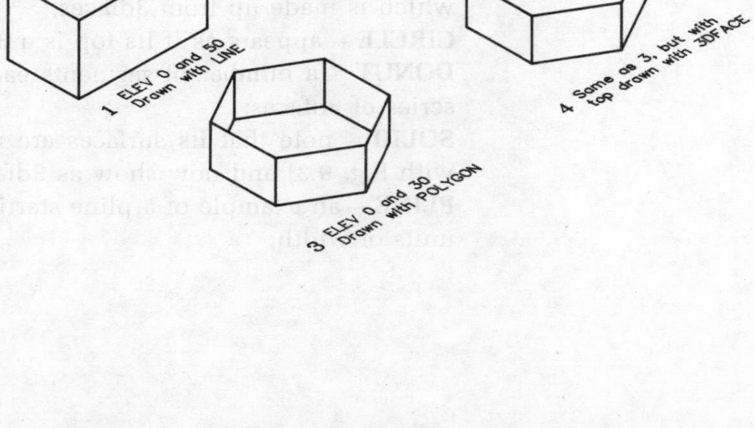

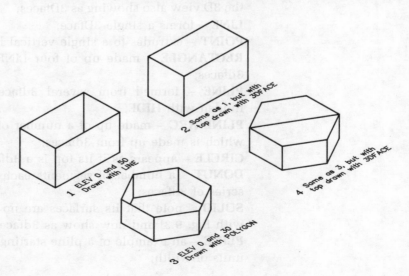

Fig. 9.5 Using **3DFACE** surfaces to **HIDE** lines

here to demonstrate two features:

1. It may be necessary with some types of drawing to form a group of 3dfaces on the upper surface of a 3D drawing in order that lines not wanted can be hidden;
2. 3dfaces are formed in triangles or quadrilaterals. This gives rise to unwanted lines between the triangle or rectangles forming the 3dfaces, which cannot be removed.

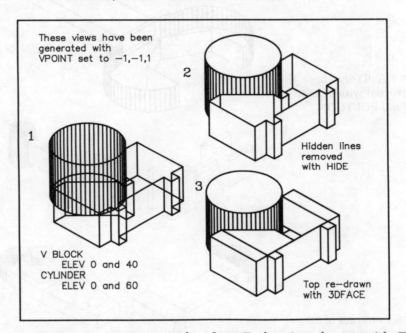

Fig. 9.6 An example of 3D drawings with and without **HIDE**

Figure 9.7 is an example of a 3D drawing drawn with **ELEV**, **PLINE**, **ARC POLYGON** and **3DLINE**. This 3D drawing shows that because 3dfaces can only be drawn as triangles and quadrilaterals, it is not possible to hide all unwanted lines. However, even these unwanted lines can be made *invisible* (see p. 155).

Figure 9.8 shows further examples of simple 3D drawings constructed on **ELEV**ations, then viewed with **VPOINT** with hidden lines removed with **HIDE**.

Further details about the command VPOINT

Remember that **VPOINT** (viewing point) can only be successfully employed with 3D drawings. An orthographic drawing in three views (say) drawn in 2D cannot be viewed as a 3D drawing. In the examples which follow, plans have been drawn on **ELEV**ations of various thicknesses. These have then been viewed from a variety of

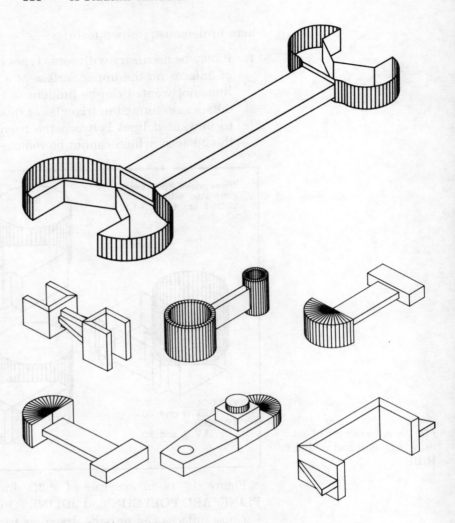

Fig. 9.7 A 3D drawing constructed with **PLINE**, **ARC** and **POLYGON**

Fig. 9.8 Examples of 3D drawings constructed on **ELEV**ations

directions with **VPOINT**.

There are three methods of choosing a viewing point with the **VPOINT** command:

1. When **VPOINT** is called, the command line shows

    Command: VPOINT
    Rotate/<View point> 0.0000, 0.0000, 1.0000: 1, 1, 1
    Keyboard Return
    Regenerating drawing. *drawing regenerates*
    Command:

Figure 9.9 shows how a 3D drawing can be viewed from any direction with the aid of **VPOINT**. In each of the views given in Fig. 9.9, all hidden lines have been removed with **HIDE**.

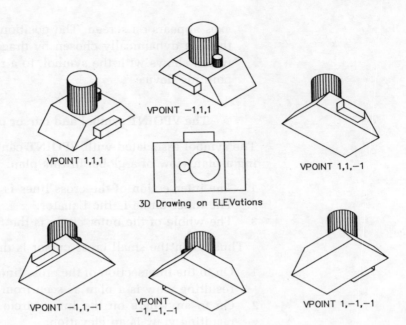

Fig. 9.9 Different views of
the same 3D drawing
obtained with **VPOINT**

2. When **VPOINT** is called, the command line shows

   Command: VPOINT
   Rotate/<View point> 0.0000, 0.0000, 1.0000: r *Keyboard*
   Return
   Enter angle in X–Y plane from X axis <270>: *Figure or*
   dragged
   Enter angle from X–Y plane <90>: *Figure or dragged*
   Regenerating drawing. *drawing regenerates to given angles*
   Command:

   Notes

   1. The drag line angle in response to **Angle in X–Y plane** is the
      angle to the x axis in the x, y plane.
   2. The drag line angle in response to **Angle from X–Y plane** is the
      angle to the x, y plane (above or below) from which the 3Dface
      of the plan is viewed.
   3. When VPOINT is called, the command line shows

      Command: VPOINT
      Rotate/<View point> 0.0000, 0.0000, 1.0000: *Return*

      If, instead of answering with r (rotate) or with a set of x, y, z
      coordinates, *Return* is pressed, a symbol and a set of lettered

axes appears on screen. The position of the viewing point can then be dynamically chosen by dragging a small cross cursor, which shows with the symbol, to a required position with the pointing device.

The VPOINT symbol and cursor positions

The symbol associated with **VPOINT** can be regarded as representing a plan view of a globe. In this plan:

1. The intersection of the cross lines is the North Pole;
2. The inner circle is the Equator;
3. The whole of the outer circle is the South Pole.

Thus when the small cross cursor is dragged:

1. On to the intersection of the cross lines and *Return* pressed, the resulting view is a plan as seen from above;
2. On to anywhere on the inner circle and *Return* pressed, the resulting view is an elevation;
3. On to anywhere on the outer circle and *Return* pressed, the resulting view is an inverted plan as seen from below.

Figure 9.10 shows the results of dynamically choosing four different viewing points from the viewpoint symbol.

Note: In all cases with **VPOINT** views, if **GRID** is **ON**, the **grid** points rotate with the chosen viewing point.

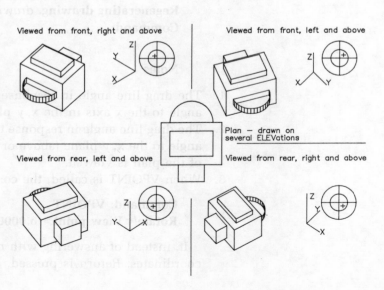

Fig. 9.10 **VPOINT** positions set with the aid of the **VPOINT** symbol

Viewed from front, right and above   Viewed from front, left and above

Plan — drawn on several ELEVations

Viewed from rear, left and above   Viewed from rear, right and above

Exercises

Drawings 1, 2 and 3 of Fig. 9.11 are plan views constructed on **ELEV**ations of varying thicknesses. Drawing 4 is a 2D orthographic projection drawn with **LINE**. In your answers to drawings 1, 2 and 3 use any sizes thought to be suitable. Care must be taken to ensure that arcs and plines meet at satisfactory positions.

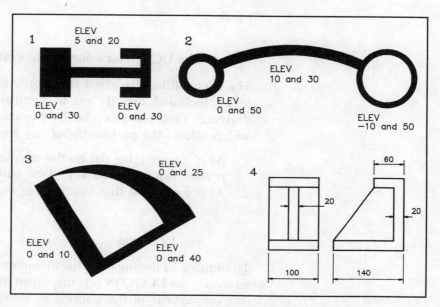

Fig. 9.11 Exercises

1. Construct drawing 1, produce a **VPOINT** drawing on the monitor and **HIDE** hidden lines.
2. Construct drawing 2, call **VPOINT**, produce a number of views from different viewing positions. **HIDE** hidden lines in each view chosen.
3. Draw the given plan to the **ELEV**ations shown. Call **VPOINT**. Select a suitable viewing position and **HIDE** hidden lines.
4. Construct a **3DFACE** drawing of the part given by drawing 4. Produce suitable 3D drawings on screen with **VPOINT**. **HIDE** all hidden lines.

CHAPTER 10

Further 3D facilities

The UCS (user coordinate system)

The 3D facilities discussed so far only allow constructional details to be included directly on to vertical or horizontal faces of a drawing. This problem can be overcome with AutoCAD's **UCS**, which allows the positioning of any surface of a 3D drawing:

1. As if it were lying flat on the monitor screen's surface, i.e. as if it were resting in the x, y plane with z = 0; and
2. As if looking at that face in plan view.

The UCS icon

To indicate to the operator the alignment of the current **UCS** plane, an icon – the **UCSICON** – is displayed on screen. Broadly speaking, this can appear in three forms as shown in Fig. 10.1, depending upon the position of the **UCS** plane.

To permit the correct positioning of the icon two variables must first be set. These are *UCSICON* (set at 3) and *UCSFOLLOW* (set at 1). To set these two variables:

> **Command: SETVAR**
> **SETVAR variable name:** ucsicon *keyboard Return*
> **New value for UCSICON <0>:** 3 *Keyboard Return*
> **Command:**

and

> **Command: SETVAR**
> **SETVAR variable name:** ucsfollow *keyboard Return*
> **New value for UCSFOLLOW <0>:** 1 *keyboard Return*
> **Command:**

While constructing a drawing in the UCS, if the icon is replaced by the broken pencil icon shown in Fig. 10.1, this is a warning that picking points on the screen may be meaningless because the position taken for the UCS plane is looking along or at its edge (or nearly so). If the broken pencil icon appears it is best to undo the last action taken and try again.

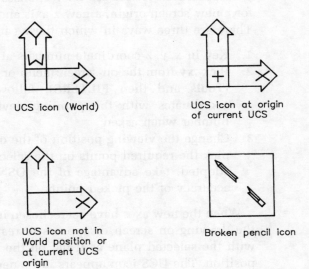

UCS icon (World)

UCS icon at origin of current UCS

UCS icon not in World position or at current UCS origin

Broken pencil icon

Fig. 10.1 The **UCSICON** in its various forms, together with the broken pencil icon

The command UCSICON

When the two variables have been set, then call the command **UCSICON**:

> **Command:** ucsicon *keyboard Return*
> **ON/OFF/All/Norigin/ORigin/ <on>:**

The prompts which appear have the following meaning:

ON – the icon is enabled and appears on screen;
OFF – the icon is disabled and disappears from the screen;
All – applies the effects of the current **UCS** to all viewpoints.
Noorigin – the icon is displayed at the lower left corner of the screen even if this is not the **UCS** origin;
ORigin – icon displayed at 0, 0, 0, of the *current* **UCS**.

The command UCS

When **UCS** is keyed, or selected, the command line shows

Command: UCS
Origin/ZAxis/3point/Entity/View/X/Y/Z/Prev/Restore/Save/
Del/?/<World>:

To ensure that any face of a 3D drawing is lying as if flat on the screen, set the **UCS** plane by selecting **3point** (keying 3). The prompts which follow ask for responses for the x, y, z coordinates for a new screen origin, a new z axis and a new y axis for the face. There are three ways in which these can be chosen:

1. Key in x, y, z coordinate numbers at each prompt;
2. Pick **.xy** from the on-screen menu or from the pull-down menu (**Tools** and then **FILTERS**), followed by picking the x, y coordinates with the pointing device and keying in the z number when asked;
3. Change the viewing position of the drawing with **VPOINT** and pick the required points on the selected face. If this method is adopted, take advantage of the **OSNAP** commands to ensure accuracy of the picked points.

When the new axes have been chosen in response to the prompts, the drawing on screen disappears to reappear in its new position with the selected plane as if flat on the monitor screen, in a plan position. The **UCS** icon appears in its new position at the origin of the selected (now current) **UCS** plane (Fig. 10.2).

Note: The **UCS** icon will only appear at the origin of the new

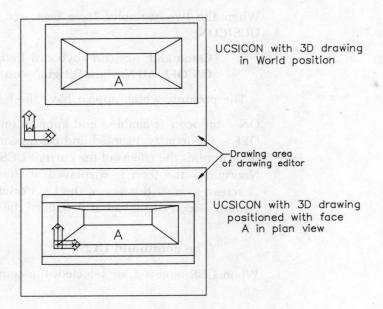

UCSICON with 3D drawing
in World position

Drawing area
of drawing editor

UCSICON with 3D drawing
positioned with face
A in plan view

Fig. 10.2 Examples of the positions of the **UCSICON**, when **UCSICON** is **ON** and set to **OR**igin (current) **UCS** if the **OR**igin option is set from the command **UCSICON** at the time it is being set to **ON**.

3Dfaces and 3Dlines can now be added directly on to the face or advantage can be taken of the **ELEV**ation facility (or **TABSURF**, p. 142) to construct recessed or protruding features on the face.

Figure 10.2 is an example of a 3D drawing constructed with the aid of **3DFACE** with details added on to the sloping face by placing that face as if flat on the screen surface with **3point** of the **UCS**. The keys on the sloping face were drawn with the aid of the **ELEV** command, while the face was in its **3point** position.

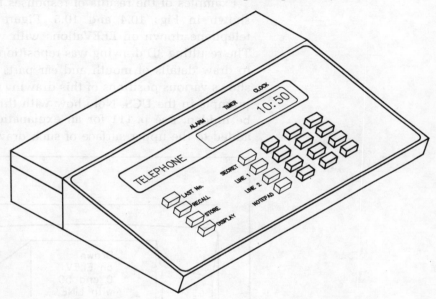

Fig. 10.3 An example of a drawing with a sloping face constructed under the **UCS** (user coordinate system)

The other UCS prompts

Origin: if *o* (for Origin) is keyed, the screen origin (normally 0, 0, 0) can be changed;

ZAxis: keying *za* (for ZAxis) allows the drawing to be viewed in a manner similar to when **VPOINT** is called;

Prev: a *p* (for Previous) returns the screen to its last used UCS orientation;

Entity: an *e* (for Entity) asks for the selection of an object around which the whole drawing will be aligned. Selection of any object (line, arc, etc.) and the drawing realigns itself on the screen;

X, Y or **Z**: by keying any one of these letters, rotation angles within the *x*, *y* or *z* axes can be established. Each can be called on its own and can then be followed by another angle in one of the other axes if wished;

Save: an s (for Save) saves the current **UCS** drawing (by name) within the drawing – not in its own right as a separate drawing file;

Restore: an r (for Restore) restores to the screen a previously saved **UCS** drawing;

Del: d (for Delete) will delete a named **UCS** drawing previously saved;

World: w (for World) returns a **UCS** drawing to the position on screen in which it was originally drawn.

Examples of the results of responses to prompts in the **UCS** are shown in Figs 10.4 and 10.5. Figure 10.4 is an outline of a telephone drawn on **ELEV**ations with various **DRAW** commands. The resulting 3D drawing was repositioned with **3point** of the **UCS** to draw details of mouth and ear parts of the phone. Figure 10.5 shows various positions of this drawing resulting from a number of prompts in the **UCS**. Note how with this drawing all lines cannot be hidden. See p. 111 for an explanation of how 3Dfaces can be added to the upper surface of such drawings.

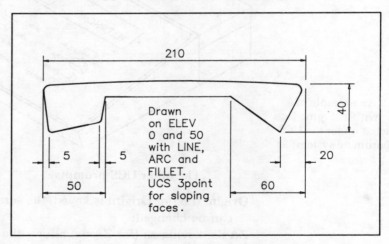

Fig. 10.4 A 3D drawing constructed on **ELEV**ations

Note: The **UCS** can also be worked from the pull-down menu **Settings** and making selections from the dialogue boxes **UCSdialogue** ..., **UCS Options** ... and **UCS Previous** ... within the **Settings** sub-menus.

Figure 10.6 is another example of a 3D drawing produced with the aid of **UCS**. In this drawing:

1. The outlines of the barn were constructed with **3DFACE**;
2. To draw the door and the windows, each of the vertical faces of the walls were positioned in turn with **3point** of the **UCS** so as

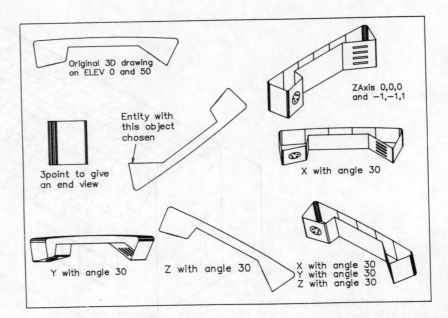

Fig. 10.5 Different views of the drawing of Fig. 10.2 obtained with various **UCS** settings

to be lying flat against the screen;

3. One sloping face of the roof was repositioned with **3point** of the **UCS** so that it was lying as if flat on the monitor screen;

4. This face was hatched to represent the roof tiling;

5. The 3D drawing was then repositioned under **3point** so that the other sloping roof face was in position flat on the screen;

6. This second face was hatched;

7. The drawing was then repositioned with the *XAxis* prompt as in Fig. 10.6.

The command VIEWPORTS

Command: VIEWPORTS
Save/Restore/Delete/Join/SIngle/?/2/<3>/4: 4 *Keyboard*
Return

Command:

and the drawing editor appears with the screen drawing area divided into four. When **viewports** is called, the number of required viewports can be chosen – 1 (**SIngle**), 2, 3 or 4. When this choice has been made, one can select whether the viewports will be vertical or horizontal on the screen. Figure 10.7 is an example of a 3D drawing constructed with **3DLINE** in a four-viewport screen.

One of the viewports must be selected as the current drawing area by pointing an arrow which appears on screen with the

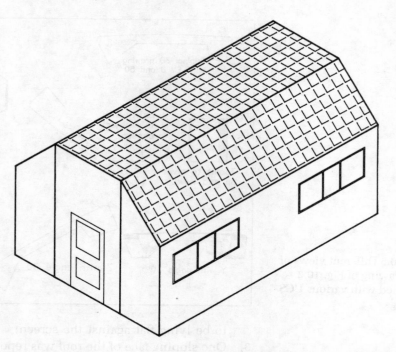

Fig. 10.6 3D drawing of a
barn constructed with
3DFACE and the **UCS**

pointing device and then pressing the *pick* button of the pointing
device. The arrow changes to cursor cross-hairs in the selected
viewport.

The viewing orientation of each viewport can be fixed with
VPOINT. Each viewport in turn is selected as the current viewport
and **VPOINT** viewing positions then chosen for each. Figure 10.8
shows the **VPOINT** orientations of the four viewports for the
drawings in Fig. 10.7. As a drawing is constructed in the current
drawing viewport, so it appears at different viewing positions in
the other viewports. Figure 10.7 shows an orientation as if working
in third angle orthographic projection plus a pictorial view.

Note: In the example Fig. 10.7 **UCSICON** was set to **OFF**.

Figure 10.9 illustrates a common use of viewports. In this
example two viewports have been established. As the drawing
proceeds in the left-hand current viewport, in response to prompts
from the *3DFACE* command structure, so a pictorial view appears
in the right-hand viewport. In this way a check is made on correct
3D construction as a drawing proceeds. The icons for each view
show the viewing orientation of the drawing in that viewport.

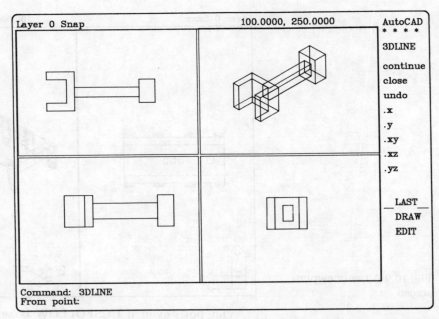

Fig. 10.7 A four-viewports screen

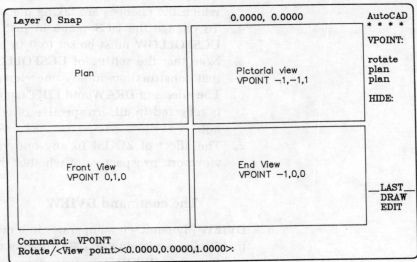

Fig. 10.8 The settings of **VPOINT** for the four viewports of Fig. 10.5

Notes on the UCS in viewports

1. In the example given in Fig. 10.9 **UCSICON** has been set to **ON**, **A**ll and **OR**igin;
2. The view in any viewport can only be positioned with the **UCS** if the variable **UCSFOLLOW** has been set to 1 in that viewport;
3. If **UCSFOLLOW** in any one viewport is set to 1, any change in the UCS in any other viewport will be followed in that

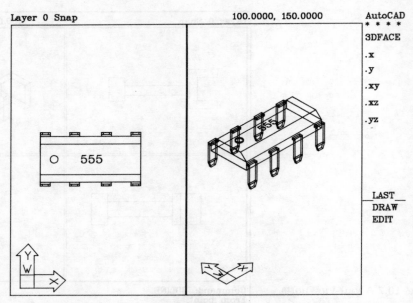

Fig. 10.9 A two-viewports
screen

viewport, even if **UCSFOLLOW** is set to 0 in the viewport in
which the changes are taking place (the current viewport);

4. To change the **UCS** plane in just one viewport, the variable
    UCSFOLLOW must be set to 0 in the other viewports;

5. Note that the setting of **UCSFOLLOW** does not affect the fact
    that constructions in any one viewport take effect in all;

6. The effects of **DRAW** and **EDIT** commands in any one viewport
    is reflected in all, irrespective of whether the **UCS** is active or
    not;

7. The effect of **ZOOM** in any one viewport is confined to that
    viewport, irrespective of whether the **UCS** is active or not.

The command DVIEW

DVIEW (dynamic view) operates in a manner similar to **VPOINT** in
that it allows viewing of a 3D drawing from a variety of directions.
It differs from **VPOINT** in that views can be changed dynamically
by taking advantage of the prompts in the command structure.
DVIEW also allows a perspective view of a 3D drawing to be
obtained.

Command: DVIEW
Select objects: w (usually) *keyboard Return*
First corner: *pick* **Other corner:** *pick*
CAmera/TArget/Distance/Points/PAn/Zoom/TWist/CLip/
Hide/Off/Undo/<eXit>:

Note: If *Return* is pressed at this stage, or **Dviewblock** is picked from the **DVIEW** on-screen menu, a 3D drawing of a simple house appears on screen. This house drawing is in a similar x, y, z orientation and size as the original drawing. This makes dynamic positioning of a 3D drawing easier – the house outline will usually generate more quickly as it is dragged to new positions, than will the original drawing. When a final position for a drawing has been selected by dynamic manipulation of the house drawing, pressing *Return* will bring back the original 3D drawing on screen in the selected viewing position.

A procedure for using DVIEW

After selecting the target with a window, a good original viewing position can be obtained by keying the response *PO* (points) or selecting **POints** from the **DVIEW Options** on-screen menu. When prompts for target and camera positions appear in turn at the command line, key in 3D coordinates and the 3D drawing (or Dviewblock) changes to the view determined by these 3D coordinates.

Once a good view is achieved by stating these target and camera coordinates, further views of the drawing can be obtained by responding with **CA**mera, **D**istance, **Z**oom or **TW**ist, to the multiple prompts at the command line:

CAmera – a good viewing position can be found by dragging a marker with the pointing device along first the vertical, and then the horizontal, guide lines which appear at the side and top of the screen to determine angles of viewing in relation to the *x–y plane* and to the *x–y plane as seen from the x axis*. As the markers are dragged along these guides, the ghosted drawing (or the Dviewblock) constantly updates its shape in accordance with the changing viewing position. This allows the operator to judge a good pictorial view as the shape is dynamically seen in its new positions as it changes in response to the dragging of viewing angles. Pressing *Return* fixes the required view.

Distance – when *D* is keyed as a response, a single guide with its marker appears at the top of the screen, with numbers indicating distances from the viewing position. The position of the ghosted 3D drawing is constantly updated as the marker is dragged along its guide. When a suitable position is found, press *Return* and the 3D drawing appears in perspective. In addition, a small perspective icon appears at bottom left of screen.

Zoom – when *Z* is the response, a guide with its marker appears at the top of the screen. The ghosted 3D drawing appears larger, or smaller, as the marker is moved. The drawing is in parallel projection – not perspective. Press *Return* when a satisfactory view is obtained.

TWist – if *TW* is keyed as a response, the 3D drawing appears in a ghosted form with a drag line attached to its centre. The drag line is moved around the screen with the pointing device. As the drag line moves so the 3D drawing twists around its central point at the end of the drag line. Pressing *Return* fixes the drawing in a chosen position.

Other responses to prompts in DVIEW

CLip – when *CL* is the response, back or front portions of the drawing can be cut away as if sectioned. Follow the responses which appear when *CL* is the keyed response;

Hide – performs a **HIDE** operation as with other forms of 3D viewing. Key in an *H* and hidden lines are removed;

Undo – undoes the last operation performed while in **DVIEW**;

eXit – to get out of **DVIEW**.

Figure 10.10 shows examples of views which can be dynamically generated with **DVIEW** with some of the prompts in the command structure.

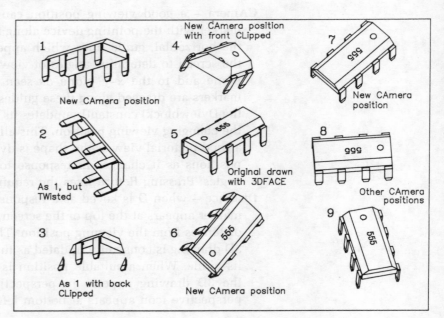

Fig. 10.10 Views obtained under various **DVIEW** settings

Figure 10.11 is a perspective view of the 3D drawing of a barn (Fig. 10.6) in a perspective view generated by responding with the **Distance** prompt of **DVIEW**.

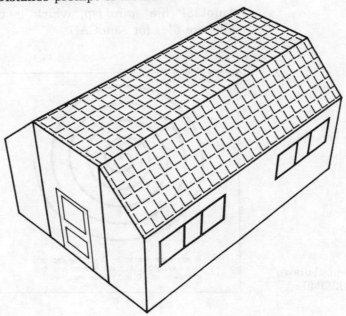

Fig. 10.11 A perspective view obtained under the **UCS** setting **Distance**

AutoLISP

AutoLISP is a computer language which is part of the AutoCAD software. A number of AutoLISP files are usually available with AutoCAD. These can be recognised by the file name extension .*lsp*, normally held in a sub-directory *acad\lsp* of the *acad* directory. AutoLISP files will not load unless AutoCAD has been configured under item 5 of the **Main menu** to run .*lsp* files. When the software has been so configured, a file *acad.lsp* automatically loads when AutoCAD is started up at the workstation.

A number of .*lsp* files may be available at your workstation for running specialised routines. An example of how these can be loaded ready for use is as follows:

> **Command:** (load "lsp/spiral") *Keyboard Return*
> **C:SPIRAL**
> **Command:**

To make use of the .*lsp* file which has been loaded, keying the word SPIRAL will activate the command at any time after it has been loaded. Note that brackets ( ), quotes " " and a forward slash /

(not the backslash \ used with MS.DOS file loading) must be included in order to load a *.lsp* file.

Figure 10.12 is an example of a drawing produced from the AutoLISP file *spiral.lsp*, which is normally included with the software files for AutoCAD.

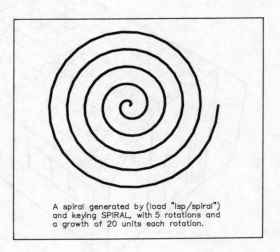

A spiral generated by (load "lsp/spiral")
and keying SPIRAL, with 5 rotations and
a growth of 20 units each rotation.

Fig. 10.12 A spiral drawn
from an AutoLISP file

The command ASHADE

Two commands — **ASHADE** and **3D** — are held in AutoLISP files and hence will not run unless AutoCAD has been configured to run AutoLISP. AutoSHADE is a separate stand-alone item of software — only one of several items of software which are supported by AutoCAD. As such it is only partly described here.

In **ASHADE** lights and a camera are named and positioned to illuminate and form a scene as if photographed by a camera. This scene is then saved on a filmroll as a file with the file extension *.flm* (automatically given when a filmroll is saved). Files of scenes with the extension *.flm* can be viewed in AutoSHADE as shaded 3D models.

ASHADE, being an AutoLISP program file, is loaded into memory for use when called. Prompts in the on-screen menu ask for **LIGHT**, **CAMERA** and **ACTION**. Under **ACTION** the prompts are for **SCENE** and **FILMROLL**. When lights and a camera have been selected and positioned, a scene is then named and shown on screen as a clapper-board with lights and camera names. Finally a filmroll of the scene(s) can be saved under the prompt **filmroll**.

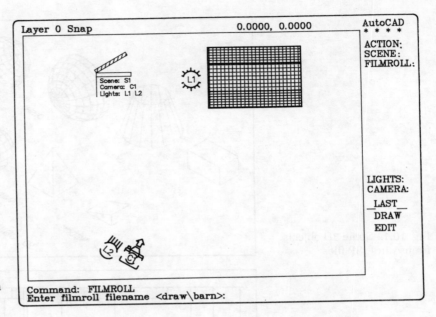

Fig. 10.13 The settings for an ASHADE scene

Figure 10.13 shows a scene with lights and camera for the barn (Fig. 10.6).

3D objects

Another AutoLISP file normally found in AutoCAD is that which contains the program for running the 3D objects. These are shown in the **VPOINT** drawing of Fig. 10.14. These 3D objects can be manipulated by joining different objects to form complex 3D drawings. Hidden lines can be removed from these with **HIDE**, to hide details behind joins. These complex drawings can then be made into scenes within **ASHADE** and can then be shaded in AutoSHADE.

Exercises

The following exercises involve the construction of 3D drawings with the aid of the command systems – **ELEV**ation, **3DFACE**, the **UCS**, **DVIEW** and **VIEWPORTS**. When each drawing has been constructed, attempt changing viewing positions within the **UCS** and manipulating the resulting 3D drawing within **DVIEW**.

1. Figure 10.15. All faces of the block were drawn with **3DFACE**.
2. Figure 10.16. Another block drawn with the aid of **3DFACE**.

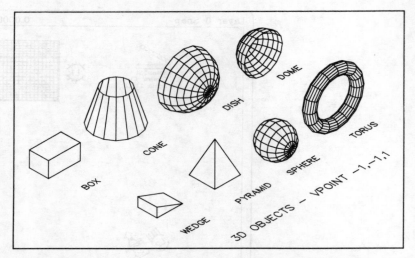

Fig. 10.14 Some 3D objects
from AutoLISP files

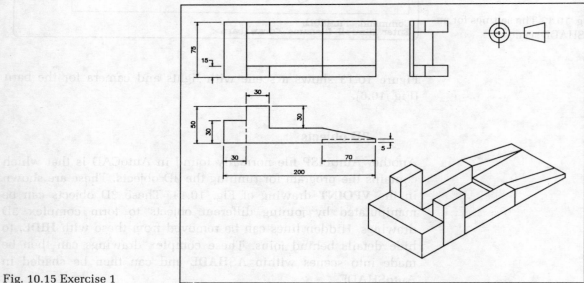

Fig. 10.15 Exercise 1

3. Follow the stages given in Fig. 10.17 to construct the pictorial view of a hexagonal rod with spindles at each end.

4. Figure 10.18. The 3D drawing of the rooms in a bungalow can be manipulated within **3DVIEW**. Attempt **CL**ipping back and front of the completed drawing.

5. Figure 10.19 is a 3D drawing constructed with a variety of 3D commands and, viewed with **VPOINT** at −1, −1, 1, then hidden lines have been removed with **HIDE**. Figure 10.20 shows the same drawing with views constructed within **VIEWPORTS**.

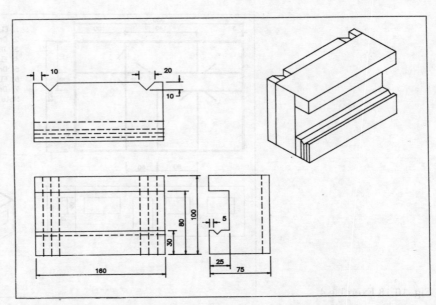

Fig. 10.16 Exercise 2

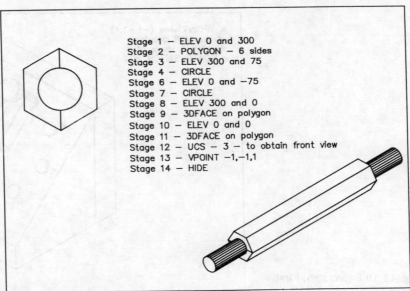

Stage 1 — ELEV 0 and 300
Stage 2 — POLYGON — 6 sides
Stage 3 — ELEV 300 and 75
Stage 4 — CIRCLE
Stage 6 — ELEV 0 and −75
Stage 7 — CIRCLE
Stage 8 — ELEV 300 and 0
Stage 9 — 3DFACE on polygon
Stage 10 — ELEV 0 and 0
Stage 11 — 3DFACE on polygon
Stage 12 — UCS — 3 — to obtain front view
Stage 13 — VPOINT −1,−1,1
Stage 14 — HIDE

Fig. 10.17 Exercise 3

Examples of 3D drawings together with the commands used to produce them are shown in Figs 10.21 and 10.22.

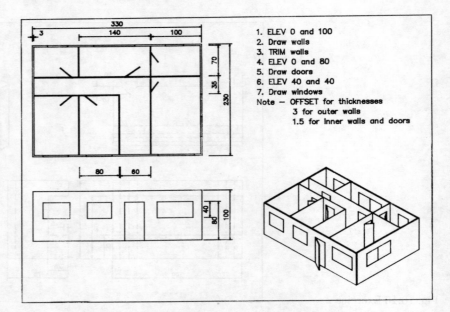

1. ELEV 0 and 100
2. Draw walls
3. TRIM walls
4. ELEV 0 and 80
5. Draw doors
6. ELEV 40 and 40
7. Draw windows
Note — OFFSET for thicknesses
       3 for outer walls
       1.5 for inner walls and doors

Fig. 10.18 Exercise 4

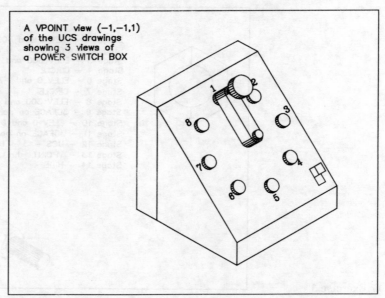

A VPOINT view (−1,−1,1)
of the UCS drawings
showing 3 views of
a POWER SWITCH BOX

Fig. 10.19 Exercise 5. First
drawing

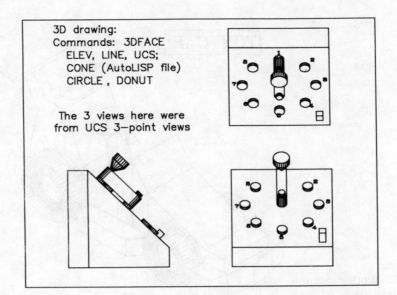

Fig. 10.20 Exercise 5.
Second drawing

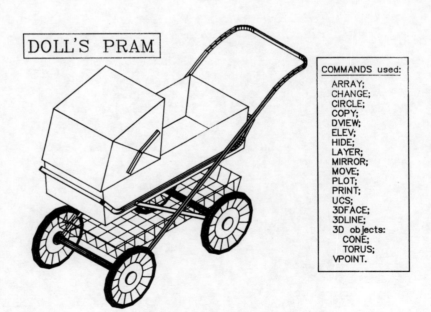

Fig. 10.21 An example of a
3D drawing

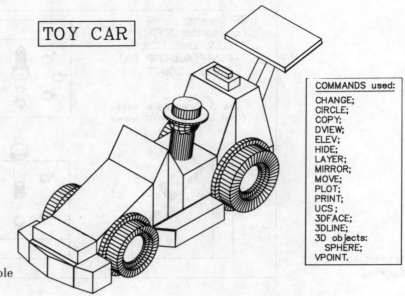

TOY CAR

COMMANDS used:

CHANGE;
CIRCLE;
COPY;
DVIEW;
ELEV;
HIDE;
LAYER;
MIRROR;
MOVE;
PLOT;
PRINT;
UCS;
3DFACE;
3DLINE;
3D objects:
  SPHERE;
VPOINT.

Fig. 10.22 Another example of a 3D drawing

CHAPTER 11

3D surface construction

Introduction

Complex 3D wire frame models can be constructed with the aid of the 3D surface construction command systems. The resulting 3D models appear on screen as wire frames enclosing surfaces, each of which is a 3DFACE. Because the wire frames are composed of a series of 3DFACEs, the command **HIDE** can be effective in removing hidden lines behind the 3dfaces.

3D models constructed with the aid of the 3D surface construction commands can be shaded in the stand-alone program AutoSHADE.

To achieve satisfactory results with the 3D surface construction commands, some dexterity in the **UCS** (user coordinate system) is essential. It will be seen that in some of the examples given in this chapter, the **ELEV**ation command system has been used in conjunction with the **UCS**. It should be noted that this command (**ELEV**ation) will not be available in future major revisions of AutoCAD from release 11 onwards. However, the command **TABSURF** (p. 146) can be used to obtain similar results to those obtained with **ELEV**ation.

When constructing 3D models, better results will be achieved if the order in which the drawing is to be constructed is planned in advance.

The four 3D surface construction commands

EDGSURF – for constructing 3D surface patches bounded by four edges;

REVSURF – for constructing 3D surfaces of revolution around an axis;

RULSURF – for constructing a 3D surface between two lines, curves, points or plines;

TABSURF – for constructing a 3D surface from an edge or a shape in a plane in the direction of a given axis.

In addition there are two variables which have to be set to determine the number of parts into which the 3D surfaces will be divided when the 3D surface commands are called. These are **SURFTAB1** and **SURFTAB2**. These two variables are set as follows:

For **EDGESURF** – **Surftab1** determines the number of divisions into which the first edge selected is divided and **Surftab2** determines the number of divisions in the other direction;

For **REVSURF** – **Surftab1** determines the number of divisions in the direction of the axis of revolution and **Surftab2** the number of divisions in the other direction;

For **RULESURF** – **Surftab1** determines the numbers of parts into which the 3D surface is divided;

For **TABSURF** – **Surftab1** determines the number of parts into which the 3D surface will be divided.

These two variables can be set by picking them from either the pull-down menu or from the on-screen menu and then keying in the required number of divisions thought to be suited to the work in hand. If keyed in at the command line they must be set by first keying **SETVAR** (set variable) and then either **SURFTAB1** or **SURFTAB2** and finally the number required for the setting.

The commands can be selected by pointing at **3D constructions** . . . in the **Draw** pull-down menu, or by selecting **3D** from the on-screen menu, or by keying in the command at the command line. Note that when keying in the command, its full name (i.e. including the e) must be keyed – e.g. **RULESURF**. When selected from the pull-down menu, the command appears in a dialogue box on screen as:

Surface of REVOLUTION
RULED Surface
EDGE-DEFINED Surface Patch
TABULATED Surface
Set SURFTAB1
Set SURFTAB2

When the **3D** option is selected from the on-screen menu, a sub-menu appears with the following:

EDGSURF:
REVSURF:
RULSURF:
TABSURF:

Surftb1:
Surftb2:

From which the required command must be picked by pointing at it with the aid of the pointing device.

The command RULESURF

Command: RULESURF
Select first defining curve: *pick*
Select second defining curve: *pick*
Command:

And the **RULESURF** surface becomes a series of **3DFACE**s, the number of which will be determined by the setting of **Surftab1**.

The defining curves can be points, lines, plines (either 2D or 3D), polygons or circles. It is not possible to mix a closed line such as a polygon or circle or closed pline with another closed curve. An attempt to do so brings up the error message

Cannot mix closed and open paths.

at the command line.

Figure 11.1 illustrates the stages by which a 3D model incorporating a **RULESURF** surface was constructed. Note the following:

1. Each of the stages 1 to 5 shown in Fig. 11.1 are drawn as a single plan – resulting in drawing 6;
2. In order to gain the required viewing position, the drawing was viewed in the **UCS** as a front view before a **VPOINT** viewing position was selected. The drawing could equally as well have been viewed from a chosen **DVIEW** viewing position, without necessarily placing it first in a UCS front view;
3. **Surftab1** was set at 6 because of the 6 sides of the polygon;
4. When using **ELEV** to position 3D surfaces on which to construct, be careful that the **ELEV** settings are changed before going on to the next stage of the construction;
5. To form the **Rulesurf** area over the polygon, a point was drawn at its centre in order to have a second defining curve to which the **Rulesurf** command could act.

Figures 11.2–11.4 show the stages by which a second example of a 3D model was constructed with the aid of the **Rulesurf** command. In this example the command was used on both vertical flat surfaces and the upper and lower curved surfaces.

Note: **TABSURF** could be used to formulate the **ELEV** extrusions

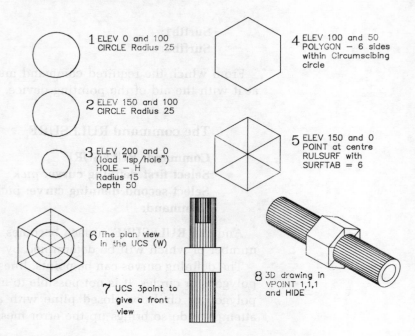

Fig. 11.1 Example of 3D
drawing incorporating the
use of **RULSURF**

1 ELEV 0 and 100
CIRCLE Radius 25

2 ELEV 150 and 100
CIRCLE Radius 25

3 ELEV 200 and 0
(load "lsp/hole")
HOLE — H
Radius 15
Depth 50

4 ELEV 100 and 50
POLYGON — 6 sides
within Circumscibing
circle

5 ELEV 150 and 0
POINT at centre
RULSURF with
SURFTAB = 6

6 The plan view
in the UCS (W)

7 UCS 3point to
give a front
view

8 3D drawing in
VPOINT 1,1,1
and HIDE

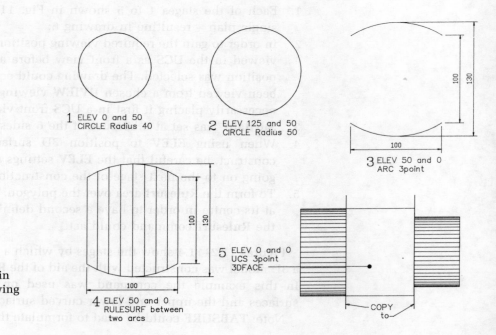

Fig. 11.2 Stages 1–5 in
producing a 3D drawing
involving the use of
TABSURF

1 ELEV 0 and 50
CIRCLE Radius 40

2 ELEV 125 and 50
CIRCLE Radius 50

3 ELEV 50 and 0
ARC 3point

4 ELEV 50 and 0
RULESURF between
two arcs

5 ELEV 0 and 0
UCS 3point
3DFACE

COPY
to

and the surface of revolution is formed, the process is terminated by the command **Surftab1 and Surftab2**.

The start angle, here then 0 is keyed in, the surface of revolution commences at that angle, here. The path curve, if at full circular angle of revolution is not required, starting the assumed angle will result in an incomplete surface of revolution. e.g. stating 180 will produce only a half circular surface of revolution.

Figure 11.3 shows the stages 6 to 10 in a 3D model based on a number of Revsurf surfaces of revolution. Note that in this model the variable **Surftab1** was set to 15 and the path curve being...

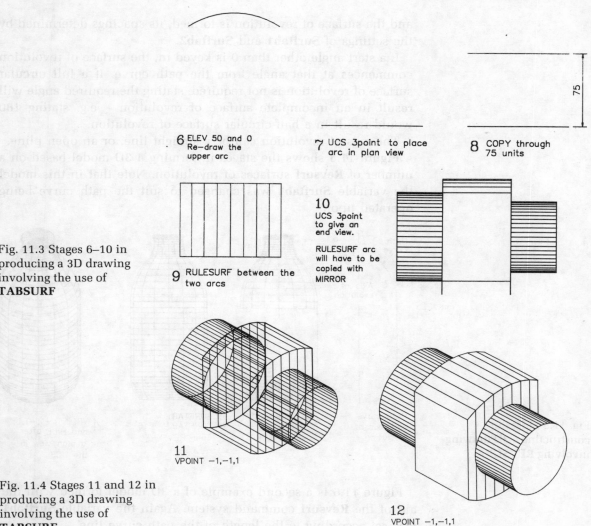

Fig. 11.3 Stages 6–10 in producing a 3D drawing involving the use of **TABSURF**

6 ELEV 50 and 0
   Re-draw the
   upper arc

7 UCS 3point to place
   arc in plan view

8 COPY through
   75 units

9 RULESURF between the
   two arcs

10 UCS 3point
    to give an
    end view.

    RULESURF arc
    will have to be
    copied with
    MIRROR

Fig. 11.4 Stages 11 and 12 in producing a 3D drawing involving the use of **TABSURF**

11
VPOINT −1,−1,1

12
VPOINT −1,−1,1
HIDE

75

in Figs 11.1–11.4 (see p. 146), although the ends of the circle extrusions would then not be 3dfaces.

The command REVSURF

Command: REVSURF
Select path curve: *pick*
Select axis of revolution: *pick*
Start angle <0>: *Return*
Included angle (+=ccw, −=cw) <Full circle>: *Return*
Command:

and the surface of revolution is formed, its spacings determined by the settings of **Surftab1** and **Surftab2**.

If a start angle other than 0 is keyed in, the surface of revolution commences at that angle from the path curve. If a full circular surface of revolution is not required, stating the required angle will result in an incomplete surface of revolution – e.g. stating 180 would result in a half-circular surface of revolution.

The axis of revolution can be a straight line, or an open pline.

Figure 11.5 shows the stages in forming a 3D model based on a number of **Revsurf** surfaces of revolution. Note that in this model the variable **Surftab1** was changed to suit the path curve being operated upon.

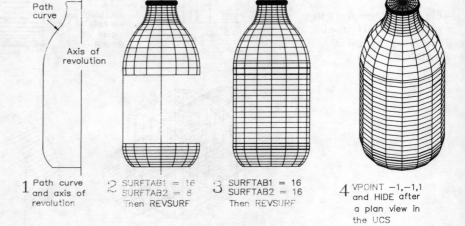

Fig. 11.5 Stages in constructing a 3D drawing involving **REVSURF**

1 Path curve and axis of revolution

2 SURFTAB1 = 16
   SURFTAB2 = 8
   Then REVSURF

3 SURFTAB1 = 16
   SURFTAB2 = 16
   Then REVSURF

4 VPOINT −1,−1,1 and HIDE after a plan view in the UCS

Figure 11.6 is a second example of a 3D model formed with the aid of the **Revsurf** command system. Again the variable **Surftab1** was set according to the length of the path curve line.

The command TABSURF

Command: TABSURF
Select path curve: *pick*
Select direction vector: *pick*
Command:

and the tabulated surface is formed. Note that no matter where the direction vector lies, the tabulated surface is constructed to the *length* of the vector line.

The path curve can be a line, pline, arc polygon or circle lying in

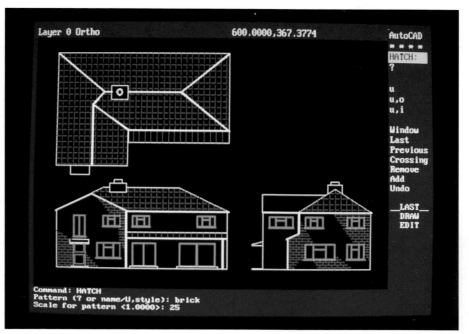

Plate I   Three-view orthographic projection of a building drawing in the drawing editor of AutoCAD

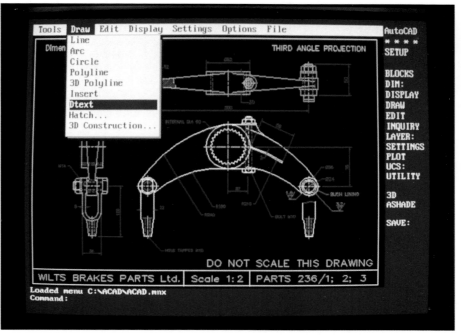

Plate II   Three-view orthographic projection of an engineering drawing in the drawing editor of AutoCAD

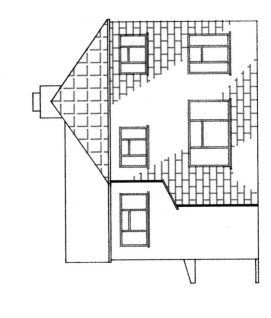

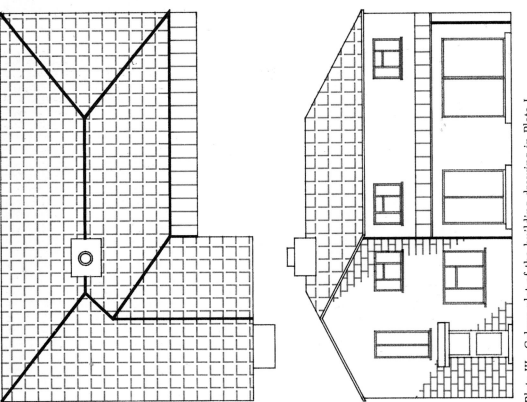

Plate III   Colour plot of the building drawing in Plate I

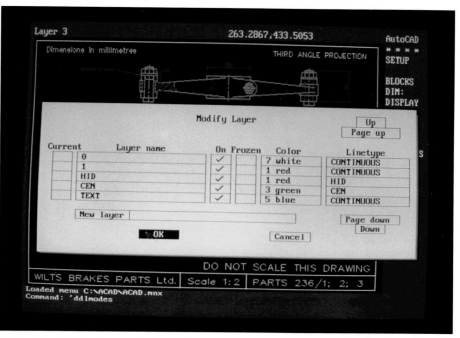

Plate IV   Modify Layer dialogue box from the **SETTINGS** pull-down menu

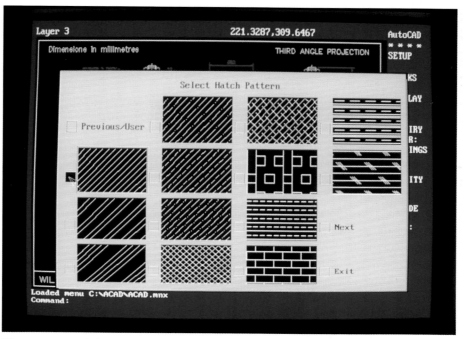

Plate V   One of the three Hatch dialogue boxes from the **DRAW** pull-down menu

Dimensions in millimetres

THIRD ANGLE PROJECTION

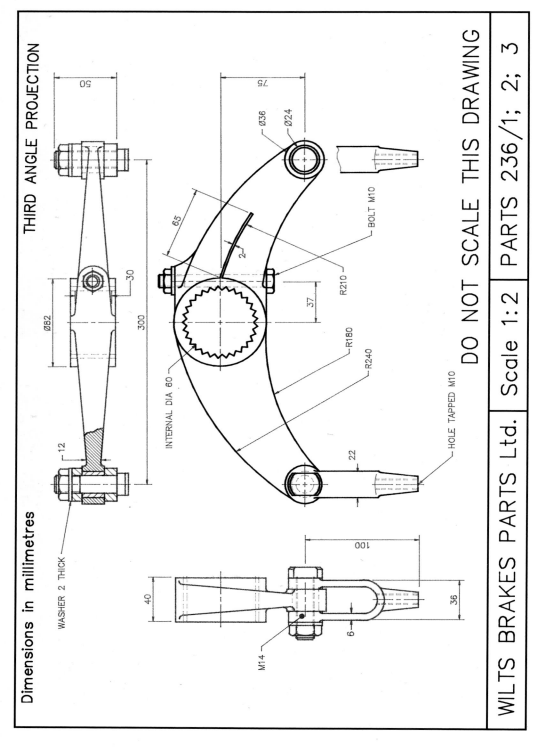

WASHER 2 THICK

50

30

300

Ø82

12

65

2

Ø36
Ø24

75

BOLT M10

R210

37

INTERNAL DIA 60

R180

R240

HOLE TAPPED M10

22

M14

100

40

6

36

DO NOT SCALE THIS DRAWING

WILTS BRAKES PARTS Ltd.	Scale 1:2	PARTS 236/1; 2; 3

Plate VI Colour plot of an engineering drawing

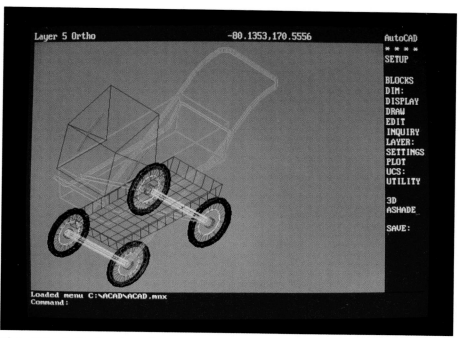

Plate VII   A 3D drawing of a pram in the drawing editor of AutoCAD. Display configured to give a grey background

Plate VIII   The pram (Plate VII) shaded in AutoSHADE

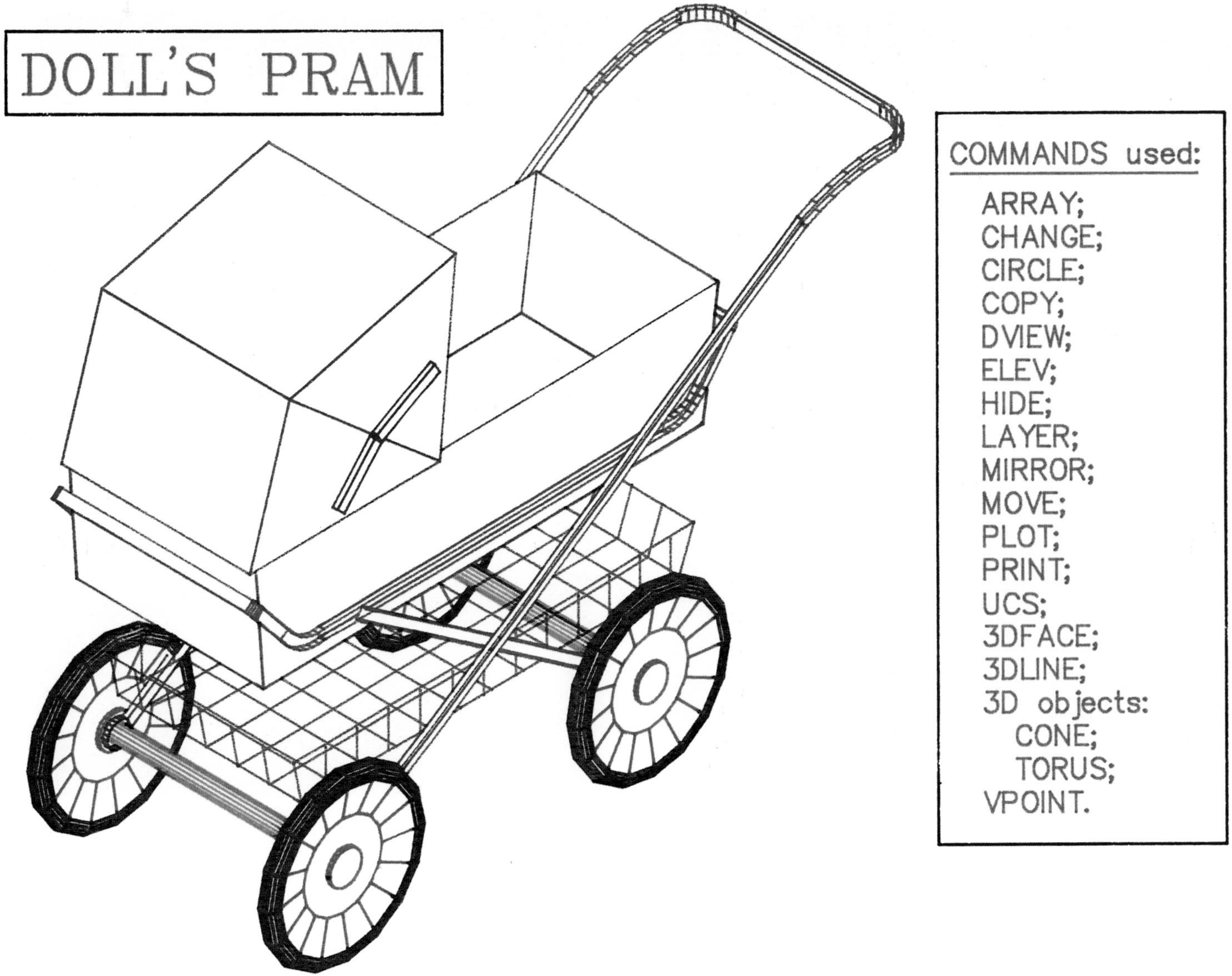

DOLL'S PRAM

COMMANDS used:

ARRAY;
CHANGE;
CIRCLE;
COPY;
DVIEW;
ELEV;
HIDE;
LAYER;
MIRROR;
MOVE;
PLOT;
PRINT;
UCS;
3DFACE;
3DLINE;
3D objects:
CONE;
TORUS;
VPOINT.

Plate IX Colour plot of the pram in Plate VII

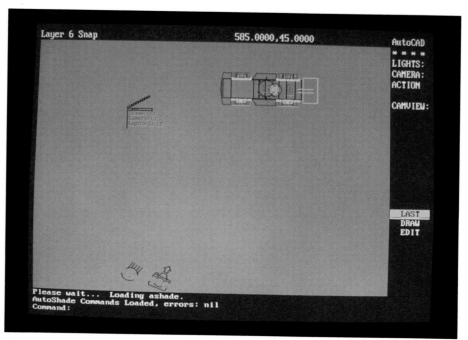

Plate X A scene constructed with **ASHADE** for shading in AutoSHADE

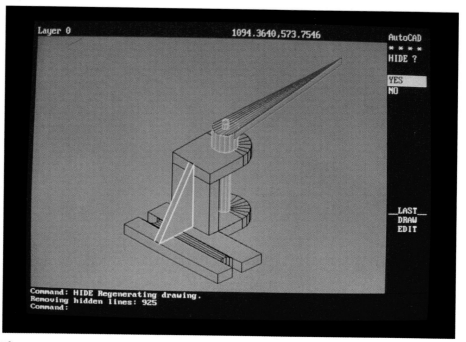

Plate XI A 3D model with hidden lines removed with the aid of **HIDE**

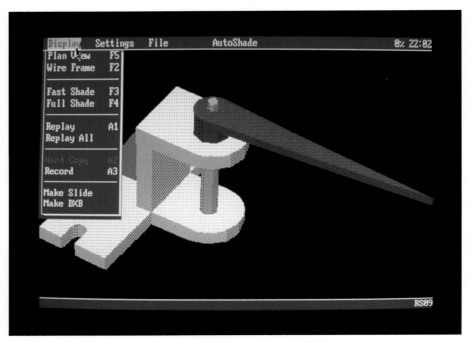

Plate XII   A 3D model shaded in AutoSHADE

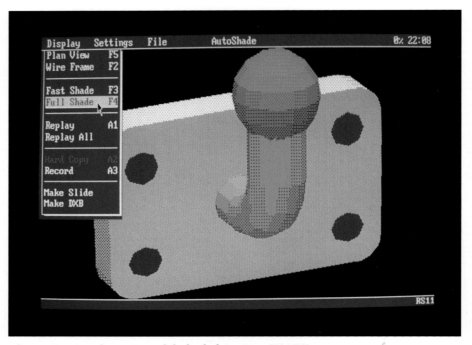

Plate XIII   Another 3D model shaded in AutoSHADE

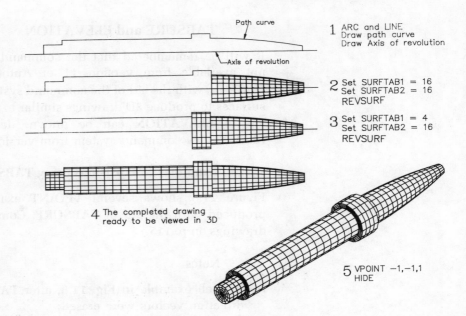

1 ARC and LINE
   Draw path curve
   Draw Axis of revolution

2 Set SURFTAB1 = 16
   Set SURFTAB2 = 16
   REVSURF

3 Set SURFTAB1 = 4
   Set SURFTAB2 = 16
   REVSURF

4 The completed drawing
   ready to be viewed in 3D

5 VPOINT −1,−1,1
   HIDE

Fig. 11.6 Stages in
constructing a second 3D
drawing involving
REVSURF

the x, y plane or in any UCS 3D plane. If the path curve is a pline,
tabulated surface lines are only drawn from where the pline starts
and ends. Only polylines of thickness 0 can be effectively used as
TABSURF path curves.

Figure 11.7 is an example of a 3D surface drawn with the aid of
Tabsurf. Note that in this example the path curve – an arc – was
drawn in a **UCS 3point** position.

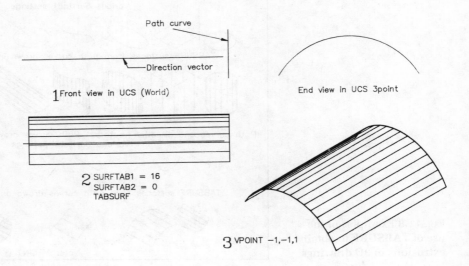

Path curve

Direction vector

End view in UCS 3point

1 Front view in UCS (World)

2 SURFTAB1 = 16
  SURFTAB2 = 0
  TABSURF

3 VPOINT −1,−1,1

Fig. 11.7 Stages in
constructing a 3D drawing
involving **TABSURF**

TABSURF and ELEVATION

It will be remembered that the command system **ELEVATION** is not available from version 11 of AutoCAD onwards (p. 114). However, with the aid of the command system **TABSURF**, extruded surfaces to produce 3D drawings similar to those produced with the aid of **ELEVATION** can be drawn, despite this lack of the **ELEVATION** command system from version 11 onwards.

Examples of extrusions using TABSURF

Figure 11.8 shows several **VPOINT** examples of 3D drawings produced with the aid of **TABSURF**. Compare Fig. 11.8 with the drawings on p. 115.

Notes

1. In each example in Fig. 11.8, after **TABSURF** was called, the direction vectors were erased;
2. In comparing **ELEVATION** and **TABSURF** extensions the following details emerge:
   (a) the direction vector can be oblique to the plane on which the path curve has been drawn;
   (b) some of the 3dfaces of **ELEVATION** surface extensions do not occur with **TABSURF** – an example being when a circle is extended – with **ELEVATION**, the top of the extension is a 3dface, with **TABSURF**, this is not so.

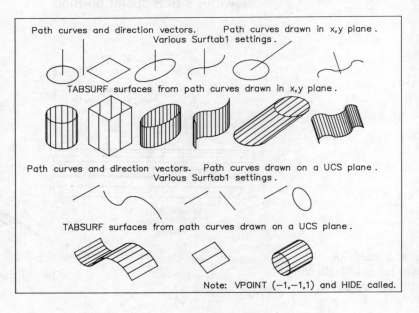

Fig. 11.8 Examples of the use of **TABSURF** to obtain extrusions in 3D drawings

The command EDGESURF

Command: EDGESURF
Select edge 1: *pick*
Select edge 2: *pick*
Select edge 3: *pick*
Select edge 4: *pick*
Command:

and the surface is automatically formed.

Note: The surface will not form unless the four edges meet each other. The edges can be in the x, y plane or in any 3D position within the x, y, z coordinate system.

Figure 11.9 shows a surface formed with the aid of **Edgesurf** between four 3D arcs.

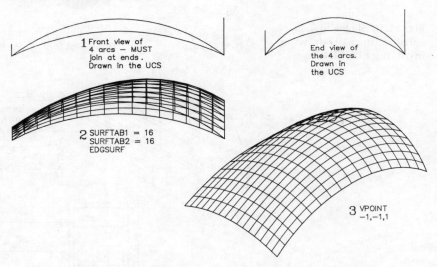

Fig. 11.9 Stages in constructing a 3D drawing involving **EDGSURF**

Figure 11.10 illustrates the stages in constructing a 3D wire frame model of a flask.

Exercises

1. Construct the 3D drawing shown by a pictorial and by orthographic view in Fig. 11.11.
2. Construct the 3D model given in Fig. 11.12.
3. Figures 11.13 and 11.14 illustrate stages in constructing a 3D drawing. Either attempt one part (stages 1–4), or both parts (stages 1–8) of the drawing.
4. Construct the 3D drawing of a tool handle given in Fig. 11.15.
5. Figure 11.16 shows a drawing with a 3D curved surface.

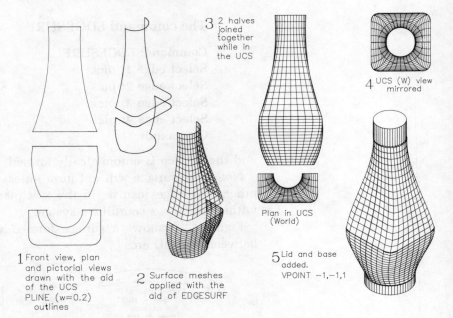

3 2 halves joined together while in the UCS

4 UCS (W) view mirrored

Plan in UCS (World)

1 Front view, plan and pictorial views drawn with the aid of the UCS PLINE (w=0.2) outlines

2 Surface meshes applied with the aid of EDGESURF

5 Lid and base added. VPOINT −1,−1,1

Fig. 11.10 Stages in constructing a 3D drawing involving **EDGSURF**

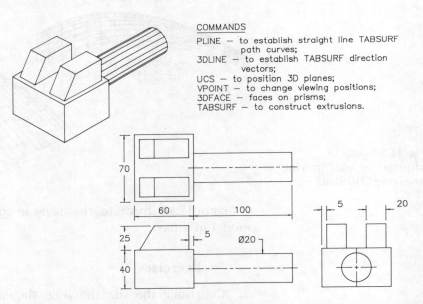

COMMANDS

PLINE — to establish straight line TABSURF path curves;

3DLINE — to establish TABSURF direction vectors;

UCS — to position 3D planes;

VPOINT — to change viewing positions;

3DFACE — faces on prisms;

TABSURF — to construct extrusions.

Fig. 11.11 Exercise 1

Following the stages included with the illustration, and using any curves or dimensions thought suitable, attempt to draw a similar surface which has curves in both planes.

More advanced exercises in 3D drawing

Figure 11.17 shows drawings of four 3D models constructed with

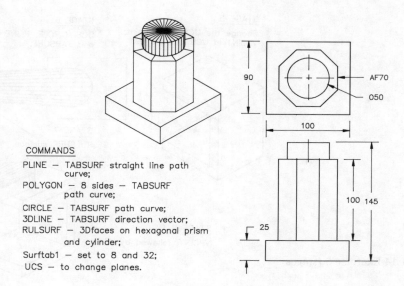

COMMANDS

PLINE — TABSURF straight line path
        curve;
POLYGON — 8 sides — TABSURF
        path curve;
CIRCLE — TABSURF path curve;
3DLINE — TABSURF direction vector;
RULSURF — 3Dfaces on hexagonal prism
        and cylinder;
Surftab1 — set to 8 and 32;
UCS — to change planes.

Fig. 11.12 Exercise 2

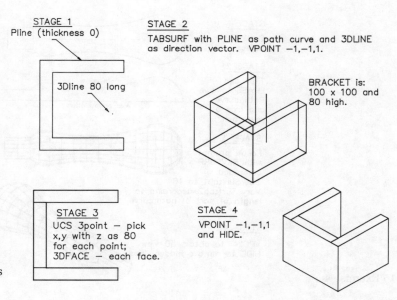

STAGE 1
Pline (thickness 0)

3Dline 80 long

STAGE 2
TABSURF with PLINE as path curve and 3DLINE
as direction vector. VPOINT −1,−1,1.

BRACKET is:
100 × 100 and
80 high.

STAGE 3
UCS 3point — pick
x,y with z as 80
for each point;
3DFACE — each face.

STAGE 4
VPOINT −1,−1,1
and HIDE.

Fig. 11.13 Exercise 3 (stages
1–4)

the aid of the command systems shown with the illustration.
Attempt to draw these four 3D models with the aid of the
commands shown. Note that these four exercises are much more
difficult than those given in earlier chapters and are only intended
for the more advanced student. Figures 11.18–11.21 are orthographic
projections of the items shown by 3D wire frame models in
Fig. 11.17.

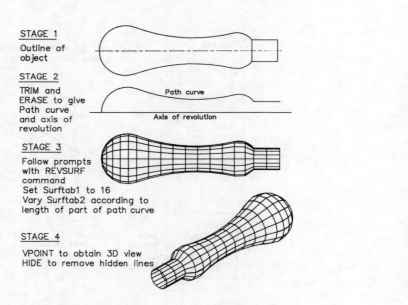

STAGE 5
Change the UCS with 3point;
VPOINT in UCS new plane.

STAGE 6
UCS, CIRCLE, PLINE (thickness 0) 3DLINE
and TABSURF.

STAGE 7
RULSURF surface.

STAGE 8
VPOINT, followed by HIDE.

Fig. 11.14 Exercise 3 (stages
5–8)

STAGE 1
Outline of
object

STAGE 2
TRIM and
ERASE to give
Path curve
and axis of
revolution

Path curve

Axis of revolution

STAGE 3
Follow prompts
with REVSURF
command
Set Surftab1 to 16
Vary Surftab2 according to
length of part of path curve

STAGE 4
VPOINT to obtain 3D view
HIDE to remove hidden lines

Fig. 11.15 Exercise 4

To draw invisible 3DFACEs

Figure 11.22 shows three drawings of the 3D model number 3 from
Fig. 11.17. The three drawings show:

1. The model with no 3DFACEs after the command **HIDE** has
   been called;
2. The model with 3DFACEs formed with **Rulesurf** after the
   command **HIDE** has been called;

1. Construct the 4 edges of the surface with PLINE arcs;
2. Each arc must be drawn on its correct UCS plane;
3. Place the surface in a good viewing position with the aid of VPOINT;
4. Set both Surftab1 and Surftab2 to 32;
5. Select the command EDGSURF and follow prompts on the command line;
6. HIDE all hidden lines.

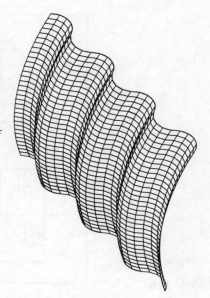

Fig. 11.16 Exercise 5

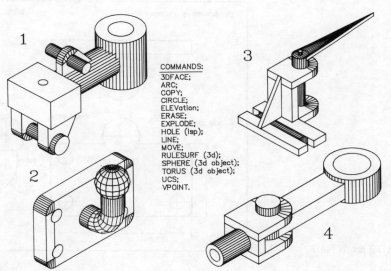

COMMANDS:
3DFACE;
ARC;
COPY;
CIRCLE;
ELEVation;
ERASE;
EXPLODE;
HOLE (lsp);
LINE;
MOVE;
RULESURF (3d);
SPHERE (3d object);
TORUS (3d object);
UCS;
VPOINT.

Fig. 11.17 Examples of 3D drawings involving a variety of commands

3. The model with the lines between 3DFACEs made invisible. 3DFACE lines can be made invisible in one of two ways:

Method 1

When drawing each 3DFACE follow the sequence

Command: 3DFACE
First point: i *Keyboard Return pick*

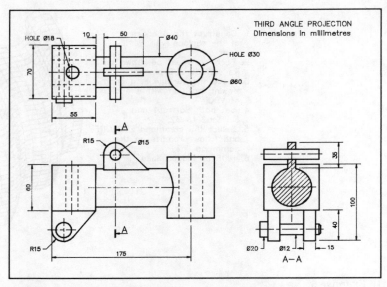

Fig. 11.18 Exercise 6

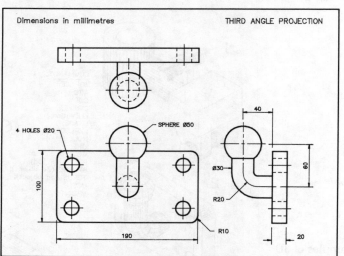

Fig. 11.19 Exercise 7

Second point: i *Keyboard Return pick*
Third point: i *Keyboard Return pick*
Fourth point: i *Keyboard Return pick*
Third point: *Return*

and an invisible 3DFACE will have been formed.

Method 2

Load the AutoLISP file *hedge.lsp*. This file is designed to act on the

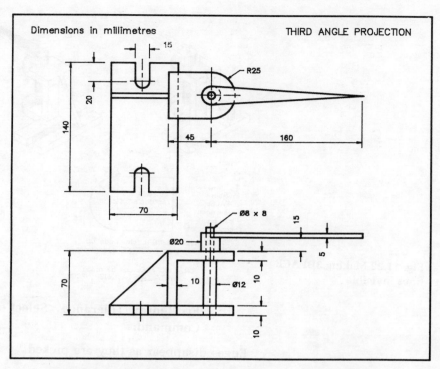

Fig. 11.20 Exercise 8

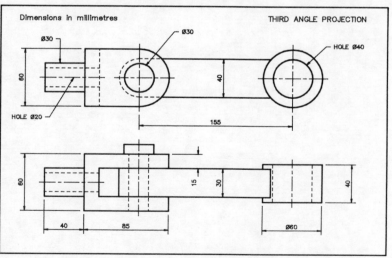

Fig. 11.21 Exercise 9

lines between 3DFACEs and make them invisible. This file is commonly held in the directory *acad\lsp*.

> **Command:** (load "lsp/hedge") *Return*
> **C:HEDGE**
> **Command:** hedge *Keyboard Return*

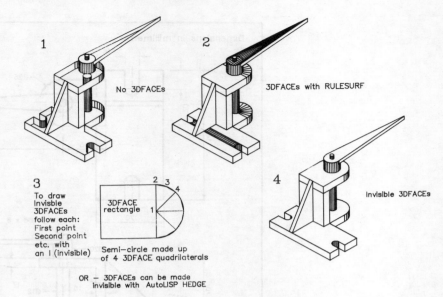

Fig. 11.22 Making **3DFACE**
lines invisible

Fix/Redraw/Tolerance/<Select edge>: *pick edges in turn*
Command:

Edges disappear as they are picked.

CHAPTER 12

Printing and plotting

Introduction

A large number of different types of printers and plotters are
available for connecting to a workstation running AutoCAD.
Plotters are connected to the computer at the workstation via either
serial or parallel ports. AutoCAD must be configured to run
drawing (extension .*dwg*) or plot (extension .*plt*) files to produce
hard copy (copies on paper) of drawings constructed on screen or
held as drawing or plot files. If, when AutoCAD is started up, the
option:

5. Configure AutoCAD

is chosen, details of the hardware which the workstation is
configured to run appears on screen — type of video display,
digitiser used (e.g. mouse), plotter and printer. When AutoCAD is
started up, the computer automatically loads the printer and plotter
driver files (extension .*drv*) for which the system has been
configured.

It will be noted under the **Main menu** that one option is

3. Plot a drawing.

Another is

4. Printer plot a drawing

If either of these options are chosen a prompt appears below the
Main menu requesting:

Enter NAME of drawing

.*dwg* extension), the screen will show details of the parameters for
plotting (or printing) the drawing. These parameters are the same as
for plotting (or printing) a drawing from the screen and are given
below when plotting from the screen is discussed.

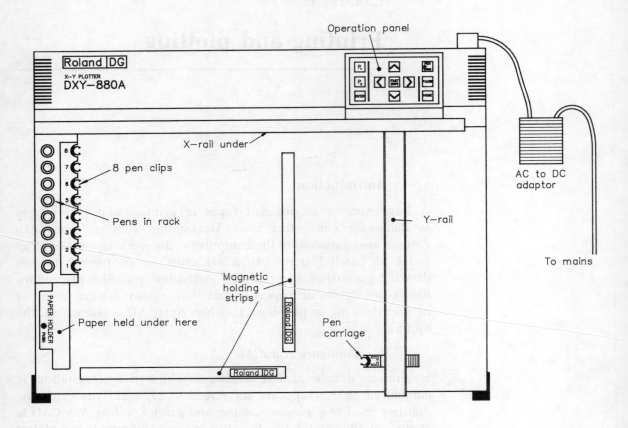

Fig. 12.1 A plan of the
Roland 880A plotter

There is no need, in this book, to describe the variety of printers and plotters available nowadays. In any case, the procedures are similar for all types and are fully described on screen when hard copy is being produced. The details given here are for an Epson FX–800 printer (a 9-pin dot matrix printer) and for a Roland 880A plotter (an A3 size flat bed plotter which can be equipped with eight pens). A plan of a Roland 880A plotter is given in Fig. 12.1.

There are a few differences between the types of equipment for producing hard copy which affects how it is produced. These will be explained in notes later in this chapter.

Plotting a drawing from screen

To plot a drawing when it has been constructed on the screen, first **SAVE** the drawing to disc – just in case you forget to do this after the drawing has been plotted. Then call the command **PLOT** – either key the word or select from the on-screen menu area. Note that the following applies to plotting on a Roland 880A. The following appears at the command line:

> **Command: PLOT** *Return*
> **What to plot — Display, Extents, Limits, View, or Window**
> <D>: *Return*

Screen changes to

> **Plot will NOT be written to a selected file**
> **Sizes are in Millimeters**
> **Plot origin is at (0.00, 0.00)**
> **Plotting area is 220.00 wide by 180.00 high (USER size)**
> **Plotting area is NOT rotated by 90 degrees**
> **Pen width is 0.30**
> **Area fill will NOT be adjusted for pen width**
> **Hidden lines will NOT be removed**
> **Plot will be scaled to fit available area**
>
> **Do you want to change anything <N>** *If Y Return*

then

Entity Color	Pen No.	Line type	Entity Color	Pen No.	Line type
1 (red)	2	0	9	1	0
2 (yellow)	3	0	10	1	0
3 (green)	4	0	11	1	0
4 (cyan)	5	0	12	1	0
5 (blue)	6	0	13	1	0
6 (magenta)	7	0	14	1	0
7 (white)	1	0	15	1	0
8	1	0			

> **Line types 0 = continuous**
> **1 − 255 = ——————————**
> **Number specifies dash lengths in units of**
> **0.1 mm**
> **Do you want to change any of the above parameters <N≥_**
> *Return*
> **Write the plot to file <N>_** *Return*
> **Size units (Inches or Millimeters <M>:_** *Return*
> **Plot origin in Millimeters <0.00, 0.00):**
>
> **Standard values for plotting size**

Size	Width	Height
A4	285.00	198.00
MAX	350.01	260.10
USER	222.00	180.00

Enter the size or Width,Height (in Millimeters) <USER>:
Return

Rotate 2D plot 90 degrees clockwise <N>_ *Return*
Pen width <0.30>:
Adjust area fill boundaries for pen width? <N> *Return*
Remove hidden lines? <N>_ *Return*

Specify scale by entering:
Plotted Millimeters == Drawing Units of Fit or ? <F>:
Return

Position paper in plotter.
Press RETURN to continue or S to Stop for hardware
setup_ *Return*

then

Processing vector: 32
Plot complete.
Press RETURN to continue:_ *Return*
Drawing editor.

Notes

In answer to the prompts ending with <N>, the parameters for plotting a drawing can be changed. In the above set of parameters, the following could have been changed:

1. *Pen numbers.* With the Roland 880A plotter, pens are changed automatically as the plot proceeds. Thus when all the lines colour white (on screen) have been plotted, the pen for plotting line colour red (on screen) will be automatically changed, and so on. This gives rise to three possibilities:

   (a) if the drawing is to be plotted in black in one line thickness – with one size of pen – then all pen numbers against colours should be changed to pen No. 1. A single pen – usually of thickness 0.3 mm – should then be placed in pen holder 1 of the plotter;

   (b) if all outlines are to be plotted in black with thick outlines and all other lines with thin lines, a thick pen – normally 0.6 mm – should be placed in pen holder 1 of the plotter and a thin pen – normally 0.3 mm – be placed in pen holder 2 of the plotter. In addition the pen No. against each entity colour in the table above should be changed so that entity 7 is pen 1 and all others pen No. 2;

(c) if the drawing is to be plotted in a number of colours, corresponding to the colours on the screen, then the pen No. for each colour should agree with the colour of pen in the numbered pen holders of the plotter. *Note*: When some types of plotter are in use, pens have to be changed by hand. If this is so, a warning will appear, either on screen or from the plotter, that a change of pens is necessary.

2. *Linetypes*. With the Roland 880A plotter – and most others – if all linetype numbers against pen numbers in the list are left at 0, the plotter will plot lines as they appear on screen. Thus centre lines will be plotted as the normal dash-dot lines, hidden detail will be printed as broken lines and so on. Some plotters show under the list of pen and linetype numbers, drawings of the types of lines the plotter produces. With this type of plotter, it may be necessary to amend linetype numbers accordingly.

3. *Plot files*. If the plot is to be written to a file:

Write the plot to file <N>: y *Keyboard Return*

then, at the end of the list of the parameters appearing on screen, the following appears:

Enter file name for plot <ACAD\PLOT>:

Further details of this are given later in this chapter.

4. *Plotting sizes*. The overall size of the plot can be changed if required, bearing in mind that the stated sizes must not be larger than the *maximum* size for the plotter. Sizes are given as e.g. 220, 180 – width first followed by height.

5. *Hidden lines*. If lines are to be hidden in plotting a 3D drawing answer with a *Y* to the prompt:

Remove hidden lines? <N>:

6. *Plotting*. The number of vectors being plotted is displayed on screen and is constantly updated. If hidden lines are to be removed, these are removed in groups of 25 before plotting commences;

7. *Rotating plots*. When plotting on most types of plotter it is usual not to rotate the plot through 90°. Note that 3D plots cannot be so rotated;

8. *Cancelling a plot.* Plotting can be cancelled at any time by pressing *Ctrl/C.* If a plot is cancelled while plotting is taking place, the buffers in the plotter may be holding bytes of data. The plot will therefore not stop until the buffers are empty.

9. *Finishing a plot.* When *Return* is pressed at the end of the plot, the screen drawing reappears.

Printing a drawing

When constructing engineering or building drawings, common practice is to differentiate between outlines and other lines such as dimension lines by different thicknesses. This can easily be achieved when plotting by using a thick pen for outlines and thin pens for other lines. This facility is not available when printing a drawing. However, with AutoCAD this can be overcome by drawing all outlines with **PLINE** and stating the pline width – say 0.7 units – while other lines are drawn with **LINE**. See Figs 12.2 and 12.3.

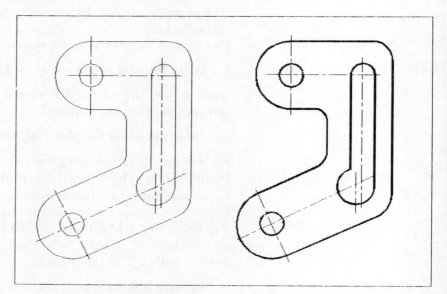

Fig. 12.2 A drawing printed on a 9 dot matrix printer

A number of different types of printer are available for printing AutoCAD drawings – dot matrix (9 pin, 24 pin or 48 pin), ink jet printers, electrostatic printers and laser printers. Although each of these types will produce a reasonable quality of drawing, it is only laser printers which will produce drawings with the same degree of clarity as will plotters. Daisy wheel printers are not suitable for printing CAD drawings.

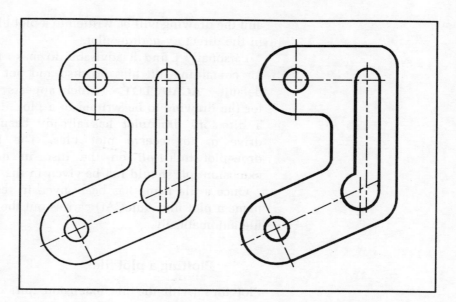

Fig. 12.3 The same drawing plotted on a plotter using two pen thicknesses

Printing a drawing on a printer follows much the same lines as for plotting a drawing. The command name is **PRPLOT**, but the same prompts appears as with **PLOT**:

> **Command: PRPLOT** *Return*
> **What to plot — Display,Extents,Limits, View,or Window**
> **<D>**: *Return*

The screen changes to display the parameters for printing the drawing. There are differences between these parameters and those for plotting. This is because no pens, linetypes or colours (except for a colour printer) need to be set. When printing with the usual A4 printer (the most common size) it is best to rotate 2D plot through 90° by responding with a *Y* (yes) to

> **Rotate 2D plots through 90 degrees? <N>:_**

Note that 3D plots cannot be so rotated.

Apart from such minor details the sequence of events for printing follow those for plotting.

Writing a plot to a plot file

If you wish to write the plot to a plot file, type a *Y* in answer to:

> **Write the plot to file <N>:–** Y *Keyboard Return*
> **Enter file name for plot <ACAD\PLOT>:**
> a:\draw\plot\stud01 *Keyboard Return*

and the drawing will be written to a plot file with the extension *.plt* in the directory *a:\draw\plot*.

Personally I find it advisable to make my own plot directories for containing *.plt* files on disc and not to accept the AutoCAD default <**ACAD\PLOT**>, which appears when the operator asks for the drawing to be written to a plot file. In the example given, a directory *draw\plot* has already been made on the disc in drive *a:* to receive plot files. The file will be saved as *draw\plot\stud01.plt* on the disc in drive *a:*. Note that the extension *.plt* should not be given in the response.

Once a file name has been given in response to the request to name a plot file, AutoCAD carries out the necessary writing of the file automatically.

Plotting a plot file

Plot files (with the file extension *.plt*) can be plotted from the MS.DOS prompt C:\> without being in AutoCAD, as follows:

C:\> print acad\draw\plot\stud01.plt *Keyboard*

Return

Name of list device [PRN]:_ *Return*
Resident part of printer installed.
C:\ACAD\DRAW\PLOT\STUD01.PLT is currently

being printed

C:\>

and the plot file is plotted.

Note: The plot file extension *.plt* must be included in the plot file name when a drawing is plotted from a plot file.

Printing a print file

Printing a print file follows the procedure as for plotting a plot file. Note, however, that print files have the extension *.lst*, which must be included with the file name when the print file is printed.

Note: Plot and print files normally (not always) require a much larger number of bytes in their files than the original drawings from which they are derived. When making up *.plt* or *.lst* files, remember you may run short of disc space because of this problem.

CHAPTER 13

MS.DOS

Introduction

MS.DOS is short for Microsoft Disc Operating System. Microsoft® is an American software company. Of the variety of disc operating systems, MS.DOS is, at the moment, the world's most widely used. This book is concerned with running AutoCAD on PCs with the aid of MS.DOS. A summary of MS.DOS commands associated with AutoCAD is given in this chapter. It must be noted that the MS.DOS command structure is complex. The details given in this book are only a very basic outline. Further information about MS.DOS can be gained from the many books dealing with this DOS system.

MS.DOS commands are held in files on disc. The usual practice with AutoCAD is for these files to held in the hard disc drive (drive C:) in a directory named *DOS*.

Start-up

When a PC is switched **on**, the computer runs a self-test – checks RAM, checks system circuits, checks devices such as disc drives – then loads into memory some of the MS.DOS files. The files loaded into memory at this stage are those most frequently needed – *memory resident commands*. Less frequently used DOS files – *transient commands* – are loaded each time they are called.

The PC may have one or two floppy disc drives as well as a hard disc drive. The positions of these drives in a computer are indicated in Fig. 13.1. With MS.DOS, disc drives are given a name – a:, b:, c: and so on. There may be more drives than these three, but a more complex system is beyond the scope of this book.

Depending on how the PC has been configured, various displays may appear on screen when it is started up by switching on. The most common is for a series of statements to appear followed by the

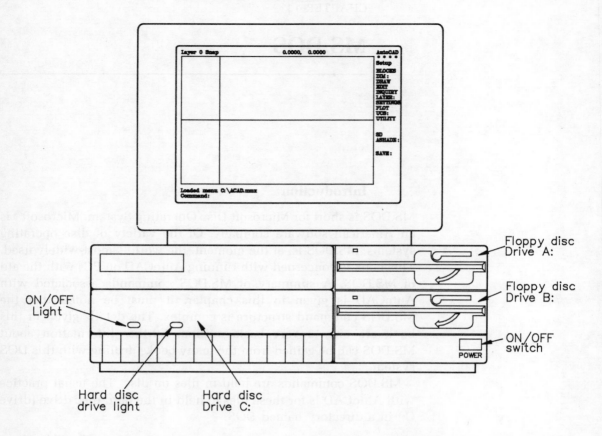

Floppy disc Drive A:

Floppy disc Drive B:

ON/OFF switch

POWER

ON/OFF Light

Hard disc drive light

Hard disc Drive C:

Fig. 13.1 Front view of a PC showing positions of disc drives

prompt **C:>** or **C:\\>**. This indicates that the machine is ready for use with the hard disc (drive C:).

A PC can be started up by pressing its power switch. This is known as a cold start. If, for some reason the PC must be started up again while in use, a warm start is produced by pressing the three keys *Ctrl*, *Alt* and *Delete*. This clears the screen and the machine starts up as if just switched on. As well as the *Ctrl/Alt/Del* warm start, some PCs can be warm-started by pressing a *reset* switch.

Note: It is not advisable to use *Ctrl/Alt/Del* or to press a reset switch to perform a warm restart when in AutoCAD. Doing so will cause a number of AutoCAD temporary files being abandoned on disc, without much hope of recovering the drawing being constructed.

Warning

Mistakes can occur, electricity failures may turn your computer off, another operator may make errors on your drawings. These problems can be overcome by *always* backing up every drawing at frequent intervals on to another disc. Thus, if working in drive c:, have a floppy disc in drive a: on which back-up copies of your work are made when **SAVE**ing to drive c:.

MS.DOS commands

When typing MS.DOS commands at a disc drive prompt, either capital or lower-case letters will call the command.

Changing disc drives

C:\\> a: *Keyboard Return* will change to drive **A:**
C:\\> b: *Keyboard Return* will change to drive **B:**

Note: The colon (:) is obligatory.

Listing files held on disc

C:\\> dir *Keyboard Return*

lists files on the disc:

C:\\> dir *Keyboard Return*
Volume in drive C is HARDDISC
Directory of C:

COMMAND COM		25276	3–12–87	6:45p
DOS	<DIR>		2–11–89	9:33p
MOUSE	**BAT**	24	13–12–89	12:04p
ACAD	<DIR>		2–11–89	9:37p
AUTOEXEC BAT		180	20–01–90	4:25p
CONFIG	**SYS**	58	28–01–90	4:25p
6 file(s)		**1757030 bytes free**		

C:\\>

With each file listed, its file extension, its size in bytes, the date it was first loaded on to the disc and the time of the day it was loaded are included. At the end of the list the number of bytes remaining in the disc is stated.

C:\\> dir acad *Keyboard Return*

will list files held in the directory *acad*.

Directories and sub-directories

A large number of files can be held on a hard disc. One of 60 Mbyte capacity could well hold thousands of files. Such large numbers of files are managed in *directories* and *sub-directories*. AutoCAD files are usually held in a directory *acad*. Within this directory there are usually several sub-directories — e.g. *draw* to hold drawing files; *lisp* (or *lsp*) to hold AutoLISP files; *drv* to hold driver files. In each sub-directory there may be further sub-directories — e.g. the *draw* directory could hold several sub-directories, one for each operator at the workstation — e.g. *AY, RBD, BHL* — the initials of three operators. Such a directory system is shown in Fig. 13.2.

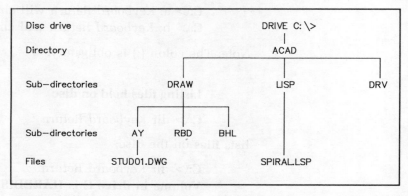

Fig. 13.2 Organisation of directories and sub-directories

With reference to Fig. 13.2, the file in the *lisp* sub-directory would have a full title:

> c:\acad\lisp\spiral.lsp

The file in the *ay* sub-directory would have a full title of:

> c:\acad\draw\ay\stud01.dwg

Note: The backslashes between directories and the full stop between the file name and its extension, are obligatory. Failure to include any one will cause an error message to appear on screen.

File name extensions

Many file name extensions are found with MS.DOS lists of file names. Some of these apply to *acad* files. The more important are:

.bak — extension for a back-up file. When a drawing file in AutoCAD is saved a second or more times, a back-up file is automatically created. This can avoid the loss of drawing details if errors occur;

.bat – extension for a batch file. Batch files can be designed to call applications, with the software and computer. AutoCAD is an application. A word-processing package is also an application;

.cfg – extension for a configuration file. Configures the computer to parameters suitable for running an application;

.drv – extension for a device driver file;

.dwg – extension for a drawing file;

.exe – extension for an execution file. An example is *acad.exe* – when *acad* is typed at the disc drive prompt, the file *acad.exe* is called to load required files into memory. Note that the extension is not included with the *acad* typed at the drive prompt;

.flm – extension for a filmroll file for loading into AutoSHADE;

.lsp – extension for an AutoLISP file;

.lst – extension for a printer plot file;

.mnu – extension for a menu file. With AutoCAD *acad.mnu* loads into memory the first time new software is used. Then acad.mnu automatically compiles to acad.mnx – a machine code file of *acad.mnu*;

.mnx – extension for a compiled menu file;

.plt – extension for a plotter plot file;

.shx – extension for a script style file.

Copying files

To copy a file from drive C: to drive A:

       C:\\> copy acad\draw\stud01.dwg a:\stud01.dwg

copies *stud01.dwg* to disc in drive a: or

       C:\\> copy acad\draw\stud01.dwg a:\draw\

copies *stud01.dwg* to directory *draw* on disc in drive a: or

       C:\\> a: *Keyboard Return*
       A:\\> copy c:\acad\draw\stud01.dwg

copies *stud01.dwg* from drive c:, while in drive a:.

To copy all files in directory *draw* on disc in drive c: into directory *draw* on disc in drive a:

       C:\\> copy acad\draw*.* a:\draw*.*

Note * is known as a *wild card* and asks for all files and, in this example, all files with any extensions. *.dwg would ask for all files with the *.dwg* extension.

Renaming a file

To give a file a new name:

C:\> rename acad\draw\stud01.dwg   acad\draw\bolt01.dwg

Deleting a file

Note: Be very careful when deleting. It is difficult (impossible without assistance from special software), to get back a file on a disc once it has been deleted. Wrong deletion can cost many hours of drawing time.

C:\> erase acad\draw\stud01.dwg

and the file *stud01.dwg* is erased from the disc or

C:\> del acad\draw\stud01.dwg

To erase all files in a directory:

C:\> erase acad\draw*.*
Are you sure? (Y/N)?_ y *Keyboard Return*

and all files in the directory *acad\draw* will be erased. *But be careful* – which is why MS.DOS issues the warning. Wrong erasure with wild cards could cost months of work. Also *always* have back-up files in case this does happen.

Printing a file

The contents of files can be displayed on screen:

C:\> type autoexec.bat *Keyboard Return*

and what is in the file appears on screen.

Note: If this is attempted with most AutoCAD files, including your drawing files, all that will appear on screen looks like gibberish, because they will be in machine code.

MS.DOS from AutoCAD

While working in AutoCAD some MS.DOS commands can be called by typing *SHELL* at the command line of the drawing editor. The screen changes and a **DOS** prompt appears. MS.DOS commands can then be used in much the same way as working outside AutoCAD. Note that not all of DOS can be utilised in this way.

While working in AutoCAD typing *FILES* at the command line brings a menu on screen which will enable the operator to list files, rename files or delete files.

CHAPTER 14

Assignments

Most assignments in building and engineering courses require students to construct drawings as part of the assignment. AutoCAD can be used to advantage for constructing such drawings.

The exercises in this chapter involve only those parts of four assignments which require drawing answers. Note that these four exercises are only parts of – not full – assignments. There is insufficient space in a book of this nature to include full assignments.

The real value of AutoCAD for this purpose lies in the speed and accuracy with which a reasonably skilled operator can produce drawings. Some of the command systems such as those for determining measurements and areas may also be suitable for this purpose.

Assignment 1

Figure 14.1 contains a group of British Standards symbols for drawing electrical installations in building plans. Figure 14.2 is a building plan of a small workshop, which includes details of the electrical installation circuits.

Figure 6.10 is a building plan of the two-storey house previously shown in Fig. 4.14. The layout of the lower floor has been badly designed.

(a) draw a number of building plan symbols and save them as **wblocks**. Figure 6.9 is a guide to these symbols;

(b) by **insert**ion of these **wblock**s redraw the plan of the lower storey with a better designed layout;

(c) draw the electrical installation symbols given in Fig. 14.1 and save them as **wblock**s;

(d) design an electrical installation system for the lower storey of the house and include it in the drawing plan of the lower

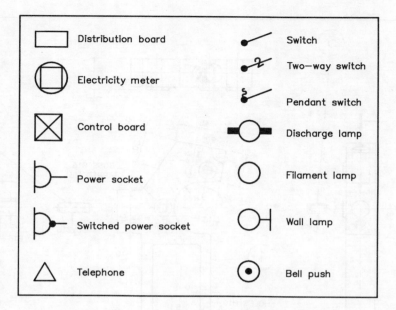

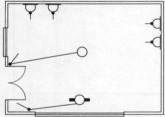

Fig. 14.1 British Standard symbols for electrical installation components

Fig. 14.2 Plan of workshop including electrical installation

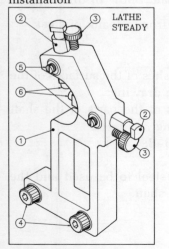

Fig. 14.3 An isometric drawing of a lathe steady

storey using the electrical installation **wblock**s which have been saved.

Assignment 2

Figure 14.3 is an isometric drawing of a lathe steady (drawn with the aid of AutoCAD). Figure 14.4 is an exploded orthographic projection of the lathe steady.

(a) draw the parts 2, 3, 4 and 5 in such a form that they can be **save**d as **wblock**s for later **insert**ion into drawing (b);

(b) construct a three-view orthographic projection of the assembled lathe steady, inserting the **wblock**s which have been saved, in appropriate positions. Do not add dimensions to your drawing. Include tolerances and machining symbols with the dimensions;

(c) decide which materials each part of the assembly should be made from;

(d) add a full title to your drawing which includes the names of the materials from which each part is to be made;

(e) describe in detail how the various parts of the lathe steady could be machined.

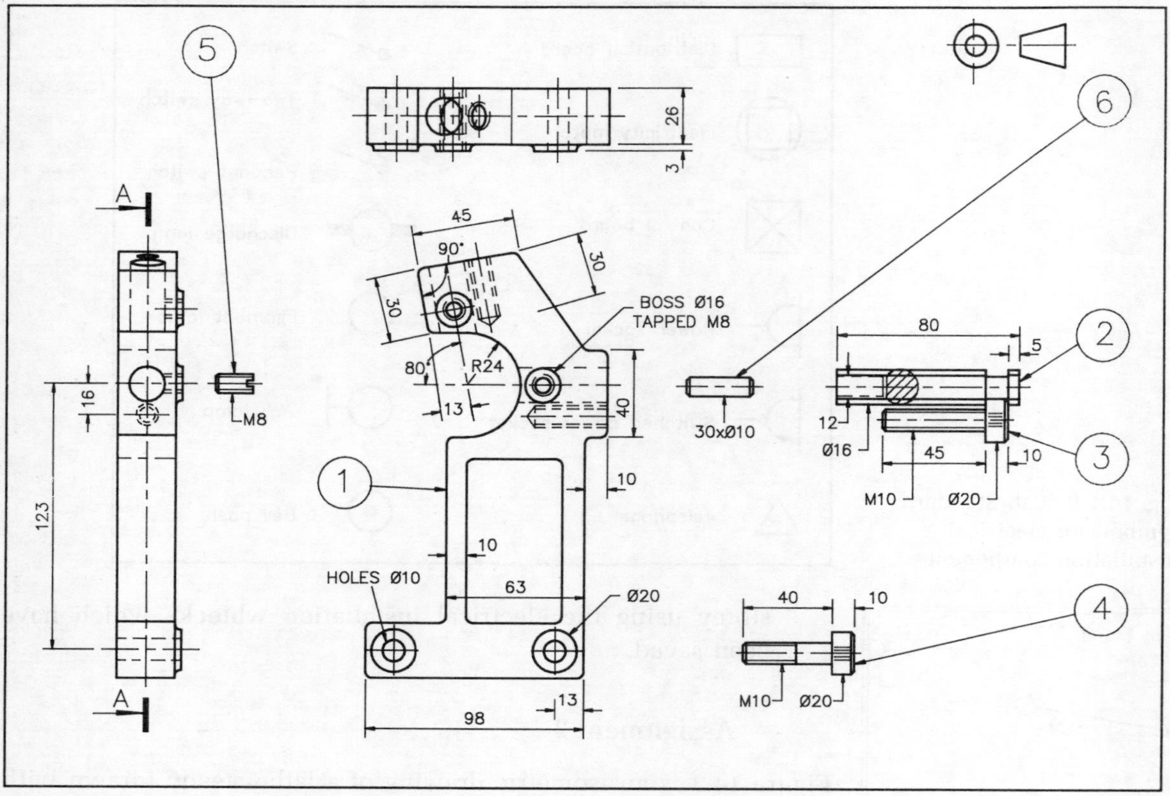

Fig. 14.4 Exploded
orthographic projection of
the lathe steady

Assignment 3

Figure 14.5 is a front view of a spline shaft. Show in drawings:

(a)   stages in the machining of the shaft from a blank of steel;
(b)   a finished drawing which includes:
   (i)   suitable linear tolerances;
  (ii)   suitable surface machining finishes of the surfaces of the
       shaft marked by a cross on the drawing;
  (iii)   suitable geometrical tolerances of the parts of the shaft
       marked by a dot on the drawing;
  (iv)   the sectional views A–A and B–B;
   (v)   a title block;
  (vi)   details of the specific type of steel to be used and the
       finish required for this type of shaft.

Assignment 4

Figure 14.6 is a floor plan of a day centre.

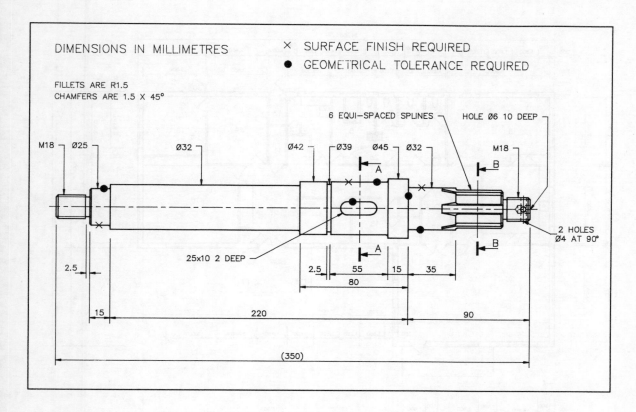

DIMENSIONS IN MILLIMETRES   × SURFACE FINISH REQUIRED
● GEOMETRICAL TOLERANCE REQUIRED

FILLETS ARE R1.5
CHAMFERS ARE 1.5 X 45°

6 EQUI–SPACED SPLINES   HOLE Ø6 10 DEEP

M18   Ø25   Ø32   Ø42   Ø39   Ø45   Ø32   M18

A

B

2 HOLES
Ø4 AT 90°

25x10 2 DEEP

A

2.5   55   15   35
80

2.5

B

15   220   90

(350)

Fig. 14.5 Front view of a spline shaft

(a) redraw the plan so as to plot at a scale of 1:50. Include the 50 mm wide cavity in the external walls shown by Fig. 14.7;

(b) include all dimensions;

(c) add the name of each room in their respective places.

With reference to Fig. 14.6, the room names are:

1. Large activities area;
2. Kitchen;
3. Small activities room;
4. WC;
5. WC aided;
6. WC;
7. WC lobby;
8. Bathroom;
9. Laundry;
10. Wheelchair store;
11. Linen cupboard;
12. Second domestic store;

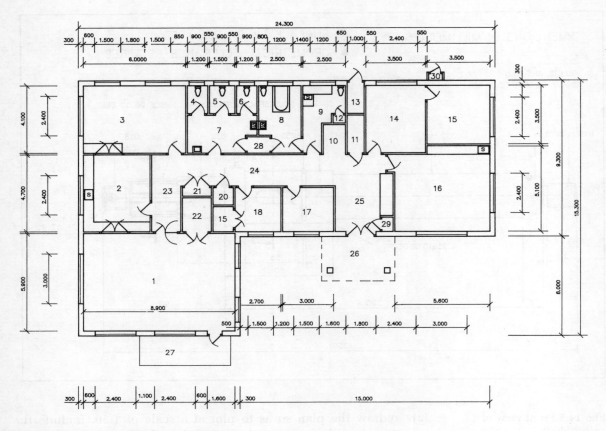

Fig. 14.6 Floor plan of a day centre

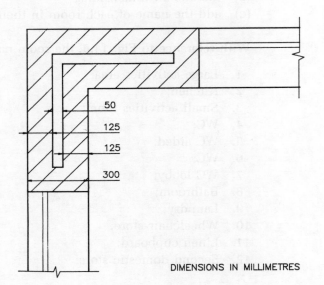

Fig. 14.7 Section through cavity wall

DIMENSIONS IN MILLIMETRES

13. Boiler;
14. Care officers and typing office;
15. Principal's office;
16. Art and craft room;
17. Quiet room;
18. Computer room;
19. Computer store and TV room;
20. First domestic store;
21. Store;
22. Store;
23. Passage;
24. Passage;
25. Passage;
26. Front porch;
27. Ramp;
28. Store;
29. Electric meter cupboard;
30. Gas meter.

Appendix

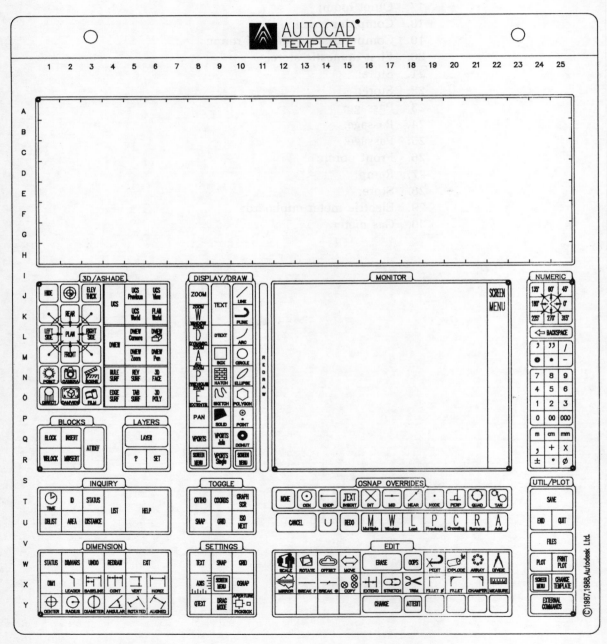

Fig. A.1 The standard
AutoCAD graphics tablet
overlay

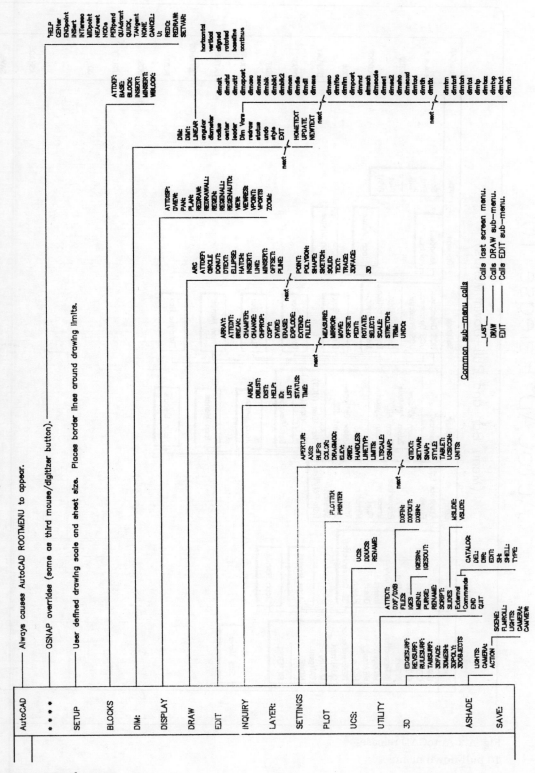

Fig. A.2 AutoCAD release
10 command menus

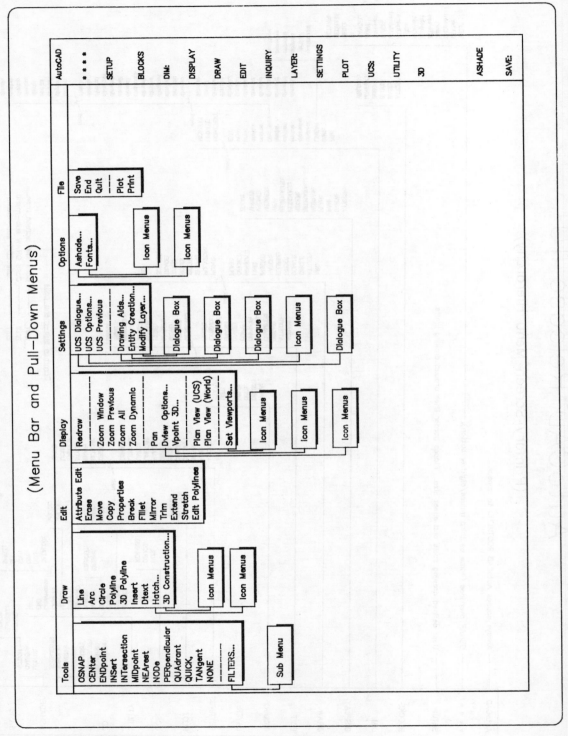

Fig. A.3 AutoCAD release
10 pull-down menus

Index

181

Work discs to accompany *A Students AutoCAD*

Work discs are available containing approximately 50 starter drawings for the exercises from this book in *AutoCAD* drawing file form. The drawing files can be loaded into the *AutoCAD* drawing editor. The discs are suitable for loading into *AutoCAD* version 10, or later. The computer must be an IBM compatible PC with MS.DOS, equipped with a suitable coprocessor and have at least 640 kilobyte of RAM.

Enquiries to: AVP Computing,
School Hill Centre,
Chepstow,
Gwent NP6 5PH.

Telephone: 0291 625439.